DAUGHTERS

From Infancy to Independence

❀ DAUGHTERS ❀

From Infancy to Independence

STELLA CHESS, M.D.
and
JANE WHITBREAD

DOUBLEDAY & COMPANY, INC.
GARDEN CITY, NEW YORK

ISBN: 0-385-11602-0
Library of Congress Catalog Card Number: 77-76227
Copyright © 1978 by STELLA CHESS AND JANE WHITBREAD
All Rights Reserved
Printed in the United States of America

First Edition

Preface

This generation of girls may be the first in history to be able to choose the careers they want, accomplish what they are capable of, and lead lives of their own choosing.

They may not *all* have *absolutely equal* rights, pay, or treatment, every time, every place. But they will have the right to be themselves, perhaps for the first time in history.

They will have the way—*if* they have the will. This book is to help parents bring their daughters up to be ready for the future.

The possibilities are exciting. They are also a little frightening. Caged birds are often helpless when freedom comes. Women, now that they can define themselves, sometimes panic. They cling doggedly to the old trap or flee to a new one. They exchange the old feminine stereotype for the new and stylish "liberated woman" one. In either case their roles are still defined for them. They don't define themselves and choose what they want to be.

Being oneself, regardless of sex, takes a lot of courage and conviction. Courage and determination come from self-knowledge and self-acceptance.

These qualities are genetic—at least in part. If you watch a nursery school class of toddlers for a half hour you'll recognize this. Some are more confident and assured about who they are, who their friends are, what they can do, and what they want than others. The difference comes from individual characteristics that they seem to have been born with. But confidence and drive are bred in as well as inborn. They are nurtured by family life and childhood experience. Mothers and fathers do make a difference.

Can you bring up your daughter with the self-knowledge and confidence to make the most of the opportunities that are opening for women? DAUGHTERS will help you get acquainted with your baby daughter and understand her needs as she develops.

We will take you through all the stages of growth, describing the physical, mental, and emotional changes that occur along the way and the kinds of issues that they raise. Our goal is to make you more sophisticated about child development, the differences in developmental patterns, and the particular nature of your own child, so that you can be more sensitive to her ways and needs.

To be alert and responsive to a child's needs you have to be well acquainted with yourselves. Only then can you separate her needs from your own. To help your daughter grow up to realize *herself,* you have to be sure that you are not—all unbeknownst to you—pushing her to *your* goals, or holding her back with your anxieties and fears, or burdening her with the self-concepts, stereotypes, attitudes, feelings, and social codes imprinted by your childhood.

The book is both for parents of brand-new babies and for

parents in the home stretch—with grown-up daughters, starting careers and families of their own.

The early chapters cover the first months of life and the development of the parent-child bond. The last ones talk about adult relationships between parents and children: Chapter Ten, "Letting Go," and Chapter Eleven, "After She's Gone Away."

Girls need fathers as much as, and sometimes more than, they need mothers. In the past the male role has been defined in such a way that most girls have had very little fathering. Unlike most parent manuals, this one is written for fathers as well as for mothers. It aims to help men back into parenting. It points out the importance of the father at each stage of a girl's development and shows how his influence can make a positive difference in how a daughter grows. In addition, Chapter Twelve, "What Fathers Are For," shows how the kind of father and husband you are influences the way your sons and daughters grow up to see themselves and each other as men and women.

Guides and manuals deal in generalities, of necessity. Your child is not a generality. At the very moment of birth she is a particular person, unique in herself.

In 1956 Dr. Chess and Drs. Alexander Thomas and the late Herbert Birch began the New York Longitudinal Study to investigate individuality in infant behavior. The youngest of the 136 study children, first seen in early infancy, are now ready for college. In general, behavioral qualities identified in infancy continue to influence development. Children with similar temperamental characteristics developed differently, depending on their parents' reaction to them. Parental handling—appropriate or incongruous—affected behavior and development, for better or worse.

We hope that the anecdotal material drawn from the study will make you see and understand individuality in flesh and blood—live—and thus help you, very early in your relationship, recognize and respect your daughter as the person she is.

We are indebted to the many, many daughters and mothers with whom we have talked in preparation for writing this book about how girls grow. Their tales of childhood and accounts of their experiences *with* parents and *as* parents have refreshed and sharpened our perceptions and sometimes given us new insights about how girls grow and gather the strength and courage to be the women they want to be—themselves and unafraid.

CONTENTS

ix

40397

DAUGHTERS

From Infancy to Independence

CHAPTER ONE

What Babies Need

In the examining room of the newborn nursery in one of the world's largest teaching hospitals a famous pediatrician cuddled a ten-minute-old baby. Students—almost doctors themselves—surrounded her, masked, cool-eyed.

The doctor unswaddled the baby, gently. The lesson— *How to Evaluate the Status of a Newborn Infant*—began.

Talking softly to the students, and soothingly to the brand-new baby girl, in between, he demonstrated her reflexes. He pricked the sole of her foot. Her body arched in shock. He pricked again. One leg jerked away. The arms flew up. He showed how fast she could learn. He pricked a third time. Only the leg recoiled.

He proved the baby could see, could already follow color and light, respond to sound, and reach toward affectionate touch.

He wrapped her up again, carefully and warmly. He cradled her again. He loved her. His eyes praised her.

Now the cool eyes around him were warm. They loved the baby, too.

How many babies since the first, for him? Yet his delight in that new life was as fresh as if it were the one and only. And everyone in the room shared his feelings.

The newborn baby is still the ultimate miracle. If it's your own wanted child, the miracle is magnified.

If we had our way, mothers and fathers, at the first sign of labor, would retreat from the hurly-burly together to quiet childbirth havens combining the best features of the manger in Bethlehem with hot and cold running water, standby experts, and sophisticated equipment for use in the rare childbirth emergency.

A soft-voiced midwife moving quietly and gently with lotions and potions would massage expertly, and direct mother and father as they worked together to bring forth the child.

In our dreams that scene remains suspended in time and space. Food appears at appropriate intervals. Parents and infant sleep and wake spontaneously. Warm, serene, insulated from time and place, mother and father cuddle, care for, and nurse the baby and each other until they feel comfortable together—a family.

Joined in parenthood from the start, the parents would make a circle of love: their love nourishing the child, the child's being and dependency stimulating their love and care.

Well, it's not often like that. Mother's tired. Father's rushed. Everyone in the world, including the parents from California or the other side of the world, comes to admire. Forgetful of mission, people stay for long, gossipy sessions with each other. Mother wants her baby. Daddy wishes they'd go away so he could have wife and child to himself.

Usually, in our busy world, there isn't time, even at the

start, to do what parents almost instinctively want to do—bask in themselves and their creation unhurriedly; count toes, look at tiny fingernails, search features for family likenesses, feel the unbelievable silkiness of the newborn's hair, marvel at the steadfast gaze that suddenly falls apart, the alertness to light and sound, the starts in sleep, as if from fear of falling, the sucking reflex, so powerfully assertive.

There doesn't seem to be time. But you can make time by planning ahead. You can pare your jobs and all other obligations to the bone, and steal time. You can guard the time you find. Be ruthless with friends and relatives, including your very own parents (they'll understand if you explain).

This time, if lost, is gone forever. No *other* time will do.

You can read the best experts on child care. You can listen to those who have been there. You can take a whole childbirth and child-care course without missing a lesson. But you won't really know a thing about yourselves and each other as parents, or your baby as child, until you have her in your arms. That's the moment when the lifelong process of bringing a child into the fold of the family begins. There will be time—decades of it—to get to know your daughter and find out how to fit your ways to hers, but there is no more auspicious time than the beginning to begin.

When natural childbirth first became popular, new parents, especially fathers, were surprised to discover the deep sensual pleasure of *sharing* the birth of their child. Under the powerful influence of that emotion, mothers and fathers experience a singular physical and emotional intimacy with each other and their child. They are spontaneously tender, attentive, and selflessly protective. If they indulge themselves and allow their warm emotions to guide them, the adapting to the child, and to each other in their new roles as parents, begins almost effortlessly.

Nature is intricately organized to ensure the survival of the species. The sound of her baby's first sleepy whimpers will make a mother's milk begin to flow. It may well be that the smells, sounds, and simple helpless presence of a newborn child activate other reflexes that impel parents spontaneously to want to care for and protect the welfare of their child.

At any rate, although we know of no study that proves that a lying-in period for father and mother and baby makes better parents and children, it surely makes having a baby more fun.

We are all so busy getting where we are going that we seldom have time to realize, let alone savor, where we are. Yet babies and young children have no sense of the future at all. They are creatures of the moment. They live in the present. Form the habit early of joining and enjoying them in the moment, where they are. Try, as you would when walking beside a toddler, to fit your pace to your child's. The experience of present pleasure makes for pleasant expectations. That makes growing easier for your child. It makes being a parent more satisfying and happier for you.

Not all parents will be equally susceptible to new babies. Some parents don't get really involved with their children until they begin to be quite obviously responsive. You may think you are one of those, but don't let your previous notions about newborn babies guide you now. Relax and give your new daughter time to seduce you. You may be surprised.

If after a few weeks of full-time attendance on her needs you feel restless and underused, go back to your work or your normal routine as fast as you can. Do your parenting part-time and find a proper baby-loving substitute to take over while you're gone.

For too many generations now, parents have been made

to feel—that is, *mothers* have been made to feel—that there was only one *real* kind of mother: the full-time, all-time, totally immersed, one hundred per cent responsible mother. Her children's progress was the measure used to judge her. Her husband was rarely mentioned as a family component. She was the ONE, ALL-INCLUSIVE, ALL-EXCLUSIVE. Whatever went wrong with a child, or, for that matter, with a marriage, was *ipso facto* her fault.

Even today in mighty best-selling pronouncements, experts, usually male, tell women how to be mothers and warn them that they should not have children if they have any intention of leaving their side in their early years. We find this kind of advice cruel and tasteless, when 7.2 million working mothers are heads of families and the majority of all mothers in the labor market work to help their husbands raise the family income above the subsistence level.

Children don't need parents' *full-time* attendance or attention at *any* stage of their development. Many people will help take care of their needs, depending on who their parents are and how they choose to fulfill their roles. Ours is perhaps the only society in the world where mothers have been assigned the gargantuan task of meeting all children's needs all the time all alone. There is a growing body of eminent students of the family who feel that the effects have been far from universally beneficial to mothers or children.[1]

There are many ways to be good parents. Find your own. Instead of aspiring to *any* ideal, simply try to see that someone is meeting most of your children's major needs most of the time.

The newborn baby is helpless. She needs someone who is interested and able enough to figure out what she needs, and concerned and caring enough to respond appropriately.

As children grow older, their needs become more complex. They need not only physical care. They need to get

5

along with children and teachers—to fit in. They need to begin learning how to learn. They must master fundamental skills. As time goes on, they need to learn moral values and choose who they want to be and how they want to be known. They need to find out how to love and be loving, and how to be responsible and independent. Then they are grown-up, ready to repeat the cycle that started with their birth.

Parents learn to be good parents—i.e., able to meet their children's needs effectively and affectionately—naturally. They can't help responding to a newborn baby, particularly when it is their own. Many new mothers can't *resist* responding. They can't bear to let their babies cry. It hurts them, literally, more than it hurts the child. As "mothering" becomes a more and more widely accepted part of the father's role, men will become just as sensitive as women are now. Responding naturally, parents gradually get to know their baby's ways. As they do, their responses become more accurately tuned to the baby's needs.

However, you can't rely on baby's cues and your own finely tuned sensitivity alone, even at the start. You need to know how children develop in order to know when and how to help. Knowledge of the important developmental landmarks becomes more important as children grow. They are a guide to help you match your demands and expectations to a child's physical, mental, emotional, cognitive, moral, and social capacity at a given age, and they give you a measure for evaluating her progress.

Along with an elementary knowledge of how the average baby grows and develops through childhood, parents and all important parent substitutes should have a true respect for the reality of their baby's individual integrity as a person.

Many parents want to meet *their* baby's needs, and

they're very good at it most of the time. They know babies are different, but they forget all about their individual baby or toddler or first grader when—for whatever reason—the child's ways don't fit their image of a nice little baby, toddler, or first grader. It is very easy to fall into the habit of expecting children to fit your picture, or the American ideal, or the national average, and forget all about the individual before you. It makes life very much harder for parents and children and it *can* create serious problems.

Thirty years ago pediatricians told parents to let babies set their own schedules. Fixing their mealtimes to suit family schedules, they advised, would frustrate their natural appetites and make them premature rebels or sad sacks.

Some babies settled down to regular routines of their own that weren't any different from the ones pediatricians had set for them in earlier times. Others did not. Their body rhythms were so irregular and unpredictable that keeping them happy sometimes occupied about twenty-two out of every twenty-four hours in their parents' lives. Their apparent difficulty in adjusting to life seemed to be totally unaffected by their parents' dedication, diligence, and affectionate attention. In fact, the more their fathers and mothers worked to make them comfortable, the more unhappy and erratic their hunger, sleep, elimination, and other body rhythms became. A group of us (Drs. Chess, Alexander Thomas, and the late Herbert Birch) pondered these things and experimented a bit with the few parents who were daring enough to follow our advice and take their cues in handling their babies from the baby rather than the baby book.

The babies who couldn't settle down to a schedule began to improve when parents *imposed* schedules to suit their family life. The sensitive, easily upset babies became less bristly when their parents were very careful *not* to alter the child's routines radically or suddenly. And so on.

7

It began to be clear that treating babies as if their differences were trivial and transitory could be counterproductive.

We began the New York Longitudinal Study of Child Development in 1956 to examine more precisely the role that individual differences play in children's development.[2]

We started out with a sample group of very young babies. Our own double-checked observation of the children in all their routine activities and their parents' observations uncovered very distinct differences in their behavior at this early stage of life. We described the differences under nine headings, which we will tell you more about in the next chapter.

Since then, our continuing study of 136 more children has confirmed that there are distinct temperamental differences in babies from birth, and that parents' varying ways of responding and reacting to similar children affect parent-child relations and influence children's development.

At age three, Bobby was not in sight of the developmental milestones for his age. By the time he was four we knew he would never develop the mental capacity of a normal ten-year-old. We were wrong.

At eighteen he played drums in a popular combo in his suburban community for pay. He had close friends, both boys and girls. He had graduated from a vocational high school, finished additional training for restaurant work, and was head of the maintenance division in an institutional kitchen where he had worked summers since he was thirteen. He managed his money, knew how to budget for important purchases, took an active interest in local politics. He was not treated or even recognized as retarded.

We had watched him grow up, so we knew why he had exceeded everyone's most optimistic hopes. He was gifted, as children of all levels of intelligence may be, with a particularly appealing, outgoing disposition. He was attractive-looking and well co-ordinated—qualities a retarded child may possess and an exceptionally gifted child may lack. He had a father and mother who loved him "as is." They also had the sense and the sensibility to set standards for him that were high enough to encourage him to do his best, but not so high that he could not reach them when he tried. The better he did, the more he blossomed. The more he blossomed, the more his innate personal qualities helped him along.

Your appreciation of your new baby will grow as you learn to recognize the things about her that make her unique. Her sense of her own importance and value will depend to a great extent, as the story of Bobby illustrates, on how accurately you recognize and how carefully you respect and accommodate to her differences—her individuality.

NOTES

[1] Jessie Bernard, *The Future of Motherhood* (Penguin Books, 1975).

Also: Beatrice B. Whiting, ed., *Six Cultures: Studies of Child Rearing* (New York: Wiley, 1963), and Leigh Minturn and William L. Lambert, *Mothers of Six Cultures: Antecedents of Child Rearing* (New York: Wiley, 1964).

[2] Stella Chess, M.D., Alexander Thomas, M.D., and Herbert G. Birch, M.D., *Your Child Is a Person* (New York: Viking, 1965).

CHAPTER TWO

Temperament and Development

Getting to Know Your Baby

Father and even mother love do not surge through you at the first sight of the baby, or with the baby's first smile. As we have suggested, parents' ability to survive a child's unabating needs, wants, and demands, and to muddle through the normal series of physical, social, academic, and emotional crises from birth through adolescence, varies enormously. Some people can give and give. It's love without liens. Whether children are good or bad, brilliant or just about normal, enormously popular or born loners, they keep their cool and say just the right thing at all times. Even when they are miserable themselves, inexhaustible springs of emotional energy, reserved just for children, keep flowing unabated.

Such easy aptitude for parenthood is fortunate for parent and child. But even the minimally gifted can learn on the job. Your baby, if you let her, will do lots of teaching.

Being helplessly demanding is only one of the well-adver-

11

tised human traits that all babies share, but it has its values for parents. Babies naturally want to be as closely involved with you as possible. Helplessness makes them hunger for your approval and love. They usually want to please you as soon as they know who you are. And since they are born programmed to fulfill their human destiny they are curious, and industrious, and teachable. They start out on teacher's (your) side.

What they can learn from moment to moment, day to day, month to month, and, finally, stage to stage is pretty much the same the whole world over. There is a standard timetable for human development that all children follow reasonably closely. It may vary slightly from country to country, depending on cultural demands. Our children, for example, are behind children of more primitive cultures in developing motor skills. American mothers lead a relatively sedentary life. They exercise less in pregnancy than primitive mothers do. Our babies are, as a result, less active and agile *at birth*. Their motor development lags right through the early years—probably because they spend more time in cribs, playpens, and cars and less time "at large," playing with older children or tagging after grownups.

On the other hand, our culture requires us to master reading and writing and become familiar with machinery and technology. We are enterprising and goal-oriented. We start teaching our children earlier. And so they are ahead of more primitive children in speech development and understanding of language.

The sex factor apparently influences development, too. Hundreds of thousands of sperm enter the vagina in each ejaculation during sexual intercourse. Some sperm carry X, or female, chromosomes; some carry Y. If a Y-carrying sperm fertilizes the egg, the child will be male. Even as an embryo it tends to be more fragile than the all-X, female

12

child-to-be. A slightly smaller percentage of male fetuses survive pregnancy. A smaller percentage of male babies are born alive and whole.

Experts speculate that a defective gene carried on a Y chromosome is more likely to have a dominant influence on the embryo than a defective gene carried on an X chromosome. A defective gene on either the male's or the female's X chromosome has a fifty-fifty chance of being canceled out if the X chromosome from the opposite-sex parent is healthy. However, if there is a defective gene transmitted on a Y chromosome it inevitably becomes part of the embryo's genetic material, since there *is* no female Y chromosome to cancel it.

The boy's chance of surviving during the first year of life tends to be lower than the girl's, too. Boys are longer and heavier than girls at birth, but girls grow and develop faster in their first years. They stand and walk sooner. They talk earlier. They seem to get things together faster.

Boys' *big* muscles develop earlier, so they can climb and carry better as toddlers. Girls' *small* muscles develop faster. Their eyes focus more precisely sooner. They can use their fingers better than boys can in their early years. Their hand-eye co-ordination develops first. This probably helps explain why girls are usually ready for academic work (reading and writing) before boys are. They recognize letters, associate them with sounds and words, and begin to read and write before boys do, on the average.

All these differences are based on *averages*. There is a lot of overlap. Some boys are ahead of all girls. Some girls may have better motor co-ordination than all boys of the same age. Nevertheless, developmental differences between the sexes in the first years are sufficiently distinct for investigators studying intercultural differences in children to have to take account of them. In comparative studies of different

13

peoples, investigators carefully match the number of boys and girls in each study population to ensure that any differences discovered are culture- rather than sex-linked.

Interesting as the minute differences in boys' and girls' development within cultures and between cultures may be, however, it is important to remember that normal children of both sexes and all cultures will follow a more or less standard and universal developmental pattern and timetable, and reach approximately the same level of development at maturity. While a particular culture's needs and expectations and teaching will shape the course of development and affect adult capabilities to some degree, normal individuals, whatever their native culture, if transplanted and taught could learn to meet the normal demands of their adapted cultures.

Exactly when your daughter reaches a particular milestone in development, assuming all is *relatively well,* is of no lasting importance. It is not usually predictive of ultimate physical or mental abilities.

A group investigating influences on learning in early childhood screened 7,000 research studies and papers, analyzed 1,000 of them in depth, and concluded, among other things, that although "stimulation" or early training may induce children to learn at a younger than usual age, their learning is limited, impermanent, and of little value in promoting later learning and achievement.[1]

There is just so much stimulation and experience a child can absorb and use at any given time. The surplus—like a surplus of certain vitamins—is rejected or expelled, unused. Fifty years ago parents were taught to manipulate a baby's arms and legs to promote faster, better motor development and optimal health. That seems ridiculous today to anyone who has watched a normal newborn's spontaneous efforts to exercise herself. The current passion for exercising babies' and toddlers' wits in the interest of precocity or superior mental development is just as silly. Unless a child is cut off from environmental stimulae by deafness, blindness, or some other serious handicap, life in a fairly normal family will give her all the stimulation she needs to generate her innate capacity for growth and development.

A child is nothing like a racing car. You can tinker with a racing car—adding a cylinder, subtracting some octanes of gas, changing the compression of the pistons—in the interests of maximum performance. Souping up babies doesn't work that way. The child is what she is. There is a certain irreducible if elusive core. Pushing, pulling, stretching, and shrinking will not really change it. There may be spectacular interim results. The baby may say the alphabet before she walks, master the two-times or even the ten-times table at three. In the long run, however, this forced precocity tends to be irrelevant. Besides, too much early stress on performance may interfere with over-all development. The child tends to become a show-off. Other parents and children find her a nuisance and a bore. This is devastating to the child who has been taught that performing is the way to win approval.

If, in spite of parental coaching, the child does not achieve her parents' goals, it may interfere with her learning progress. Even before she has started school, early failure may condition her to consider learning scary, something to shy away from.

Whatever gains there are become unimportant. The losses can be irrevocable. The baby forfeits the comfortable, easy relationship with parents that helps her feel at home with her emerging self, confident in her early relationships with children and grownups, ready for the normal demands of her daily life as it unfolds.

You will lose the delight of watching the constantly

changing display of talents, styles, interests, strengths, vulnerabilities, achievements, as she develops and becomes a person in the shelter of your benign guidance, admiration, and support.

Given relatively normal circumstances, children will grow mentally as well as physically, socially, and emotionally. Mechanical tinkering, manipulation of the physical environment, stepped-up injections of this and that—from vitamins to proteins to light shows in the crib and name tags on the furniture—may teach her to read without understanding what she's reading, but they do not and cannot overcome the basic developmental calendar for humans.

How well a child turns out as an adult—not just what she *can* do, but what she actually accomplishes, how well she functions—depends on the qualities of mind, body, and temperament she comes with and how she values the way she is.

The child who starts life with as little pressure and strain and as much comfort and satisfaction as possible has a true head start in development. Undue pressure often causes conflict and uncertainty that will interfere with the spontaneous drive to grow and master. Recognizing a child's particular temperamental needs and learning to respond appropriately in the early months will make life easier for both you and her during all the childhood years to come.

Get used to your baby. Her personality, even in the early weeks, is definite and real. It *does* make a difference. Pay attention to it.

In the New York Longitudinal Study of temperamental individuality we established nine major categories of behavior in which differences of temperament express themselves. As we describe them, you will see how these differences might influence the way you react to and care for a baby or small child.

16

1. **ACTIVITY.** Some babies lie almost motionless. They move quietly and slowly when they move at all. Others are rarely at rest. You can judge a baby's activity level after the first few days of life.

Highly active newborns will push their way up to the top of their bassinets until their heads bump against the top. Obviously that makes them uncomfortable. They need readjusting now and then. They will kick off their covers unless very tightly wrapped and they certainly will be uncomfortable swaddled. They need to be checked and covered in cold weather. Quiet babies may never need to be touched between feedings.

2. **REGULARITY.** Some little babies seem to have a built-in clock, with immutable alarm settings that dictate when to sleep, when to wake, when to eat, when to stop, when to cry and have bowel movements. At the opposite extreme there are babies who never do anything at the same time twice. The irregulars are exhausting, puzzling. They frustrate parents, who begin to feel there's something wrong with them that makes their children so hard to satisfy. Beware of this reaction if your baby happens to be the one in ten with a poor sense of time. The irregular baby needs to be taught a schedule that suits family life. She may protest loudly, if she also happens to be slow to adjust, negative, and intense in mood, but don't take it personally. Stick to your schedule, within reason, despite her protests and she'll gradually (in a few days) settle down.

3. **APPROACH/WITHDRAWAL.** You can judge a baby's place on this scale by the way she reacts to the routine events of early life. In common ordinary parlance, some babies seem to welcome what you do for them. Some seem annoyed by any intrusion on their private lives. Some

17

seem outgoing. Some seem withdrawn. Speaking in strictly behavioral terms, the "approaching" baby is enthusiastic or at least agreeable about dressing, diapering, the first bath, first juice, and so on. The "withdrawing" baby's immediate reaction is to draw back, physically. It's more fun when your baby seems enthusiastic about everything new that happens to her. It's rewarding and satisfying to see your new child reach out and appear pleased with what you do. However, don't get the notion that a baby is unfriendly or unpleasant just because she is slower to warm up than her brother or the neighbor's baby is. Try to have patience with her ways and you'll find she can be delightful, too, in her own good time.

4. **ADAPTABILITY.** Certain temperamental qualities often go together. Babies who accept or even reach out to new experience are usually fairly adaptable, too. Changes in routine don't bother them. They are thus fairly easy to take care of. They adapt to you, unless your demands are really outrageous. The child who seems leery of new experience generally adapts more slowly. However, if you keep trying and testing, she'll gradually relax and adjust. For example, introduce new food in tiny amounts. Don't stuff it into her. Give her time to reflect between tastes. If she reacts to the second taste with extreme consternation, stop trying. Make a fresh start the following day.

5. **SENSORY THRESHOLD.** Some babies will sleep through screaming neighbors, banging doors, ringing bells, bumps and jolts to crib or carriage. They'll swallow down their bitter medicine, unblinking. They don't even seem to mind their shots particularly. They have a high sensory threshold. That is, they are less sensitive in all ways than babies with low sensory thresholds, who shudder at the taste

of a drop of medicine in a spoonful of their favorite food, cry when soiled or wet, wake—almost literally—at the sound of a pin dropping, and cry when a diaper pin hits them.

Not long ago Dr. William Carey, a Philadelphia pediatrician, found that babies who are colicky, fretful, and restive during the night are significantly more sensitive than the sound sleepers. This is a good thing for you to know. When a baby is hard to comfort and wakes and remains restless through the night, parents' natural reaction is to try harder. They keep offering food, keep rocking, patting. Actually, on the basis of Carey's findings, and our own experience, the most effective response is to give less attention, rather than more. Try not to stimulate or excite the wakeful, colicky baby at bedtime. Hold, and talk, and comfort, but don't toss her around and make her giggle too much. Soothe, don't rouse. Make her sleeping place as quiet and restful as possible. If she cries, check to see that she's dry and comfortable. If she continues crying, pat her, don't hold or rock. If she keeps crying, try not to hear. Heartless as this sounds, it is actually most considerate in the long run. The sensitive baby can learn to sleep or at least rest quietly. Of course, you have to use your own sense and sensitivity to decide how long you can allow a very young baby to cry it out.

6. **MOOD: POSITIVE/NEGATIVE.** Positive babies are "uppers." Negative babies are "downers." Positive children wake up cooing. They vocalize to themselves as soon as they learn how. Negative babies wake up crying from newborn days right through to nursery school. The positive child likes the rain because it gives her a chance to carry her new umbrella or wear her yellow boots. The negative child says "Not again" when she gets ice cream for dessert or an invitation to the circus.

7. **INTENSITY.** This measures children's reactions. The more intense a negative baby, the more difficult she is to deal with. She cries louder, she kicks harder. The more intense the positive baby, the more appealing she may be, to many. If she likes you, you'll know it. She hugs her party guests. She bursts with affection. She's the kind of child teachers love. She's a grandparents' delight, while the intensely *negative* child turns people off. She never seems *really* pleased with anyone or anything. However, she can be taught to be cordial and she may have some valuable compensating graces. For example, she will endear herself by her intense conscientiousness about things she is interested in, such as schoolwork, sports, or a hobby.

8 and 9. **DISTRACTIBILITY and PERSISTENCE.** You can see how it might be easy to recognize these qualities in children by the time they are ready for school. You may find it surprising to learn that you can also spot them in young babies.

Distractibility

Some babies, even sensitive ones, will nurse through all kinds of distracting happenings—doors shutting, lights going on or off, furniture being moved around, strange voices, new faces, laughter. Others let go of the nipple at the slightest extraneous sight or sound. You can easily regain their attention, but you will as easily lose it at the next diversion. Lots of people will tell you to train your baby to eat and sleep through everything. "You don't want to have to walk on eggs," they'll say.

We find, however, that it pays to respect a child's temperamental needs. You can feed the distractible baby in half the time and enjoy her twice as much if you feed her in a quiet place, where you're by yourselves.

Persistence

The persistent child might be said to have a one-track mind. The persistent child cries, laughs, eats, plays persistently. If she's also cheerful she will be a joy, in some respects. When she wakes in the morning she will coo happily or play with her fingers until hunger simply overwhelms her. Later on, you can settle her comfortably with her favorite toys and be pretty sure of an hour of undisturbed work or reading. Of course, there may be a gloomy side. She may turn out to be the child you can't ever depend on to be ready for school, meals, or bed on time. She may have to be carefully coached to drop what she's doing and move on to the next item on the agenda. If you know she's not defying you on purpose, you'll find the coaching easier.

The persistent baby will concentrate longer on getting her hand to her mouth, trying to grasp the rattle tied to her bassinet. She'll crawl more to get to the red square on the rug, or the teddy bear someone is holding out to her. She'll be harder to keep out of danger—if danger attracts her. She will run into the street after her ball, unaware of oncoming traffic. Her one-track mind tends to overlook what appear to her as irrelevancies, unless she is *persistently* and *consistently* reminded to take heed.

Here is a very simplified version of the questionnaire we used to identify temperamental differences in the babies we studied. You might find it interesting and perhaps helpful as a kind of *general* guide to help you figure out the kind of baby your daughter tends to be. It will certainly be an interesting document for you to look back on later. It will be fun to see whether the characteristics you find are still recognizable when your daughter is ten or fifteen, or even when she is a grownup.

If both parents fill out the questionnaire together it will enhance your mutual understanding of your daughter, as well as being fun. Don't take the questionnaire *too* seriously. We don't pretend that it will have the scientific accuracy of the full-length form used in the study. Score two or three times in the first several weeks, when behavior is quite labile, until you find that you are getting the same results every time.

Before you begin, some advice and a warning. Have a good time! Take it easy! Stop, look, and listen! We launched our study of individual behavior and development in the hope that our findings might disabuse parents of the idea that they could make their babies perfect. We wanted to make parenting *easier* and more *human*. Knowing your baby won't make you *perfect* parents, but it may help you to accept your own as well as your baby's imperfections, and thus lead to easier parent-child relations and happier parenthood.

TEST FOR TEMPERAMENT

1. Activity Level

When you change your baby's diapers or bathe her, does she wiggle and kick so much that it is hard to hold her? Does she move about so much in her crib that she uncovers herself? Does she lie quietly, so that dressing and bathing her are easy? Do you find her about where you left her in her bed when you check during her naps?

Wiggles and kicks = High activity level
In between = Moderate activity level
Lies quite still = Low activity level

2. Regularity

Does your baby sleep and wake at approximately the same times (within half an hour) day after day? Does she get hungry and have bowel movements at fairly predictable times?

Yes = Regular
On the whole = Variable
No = Irregular

3. Approach/Withdrawal

How does she react to new experiences: a different bed, new bathtub, first food, new foods, new people? Does she

23

accept changes as if they were old stuff? Or does she draw back, resist, and fuss the first time?

Immediate acceptance = High approach
It varies = Variable
Immediate rejection = High withdrawal

4. Adaptability

If she tends to reject change (new experiences) on the first go-round, how long does it take her to adapt? A few repetitions or a few days? A long time—several weeks, or many repetitions (six to twelve)?

Short time and few repetitions = Quick to adapt
In between = Moderate rate of adaptability
Long time, many repetitions = Slow adaptability

5. Sensory Threshold

Does she seem to notice very slight changes in temperature, flavor, smells, textures, small changes in her visual environment? Does it take substantial change in her surroundings for her to react?

Slight stimulus = Low threshold
In between = Moderate threshold
Substantial stimulus = High threshold

6. Mood

When awake, is she usually contented? Fussing or crying?

Contented = Positive mood
It varies = Midpoint
Fussy or crying = Negative

7. Intensity of Expression

When contented, does she smile and coo or does she giggle and vocalize lustily? When discontented, does she fuss or bellow?

Giggles lustily and bellows = High intensity
In between = Moderate intensity
Smiles and fusses = Low intensity

8. Distractibility

When your baby is eating, looking at a mobile, trying to get her hand into her mouth, or playing with her blanket, does she drop what she is doing when she hears a slight noise, or when someone comes near her, and turn her attention to the new stimulus, whatever it may be? Can you regain her attention by singing, or talking, or touching the nipple to her lips? Or is it hard to divert her from whatever she is involved with at the moment?

Easily diverted = High distractibility
In between = Moderate distractibility
Hard to distract = Low distractibility

9. Persistence/Attention Span

Does your baby spend a long time gazing at the pattern on her crib liner? Trying to get her hands to her mouth? Kicking off a cover? If you interrupt what she is doing for some reason, does she go back to the first activity, whatever it is, or forget about it?

Spends a long time on one = Long attention span
activity/returns to it when   and high persistence
interrupted

Sticks at things fairly long/ may or may not go back to them after interruption	= Moderate attention span and persistence
Spends little time at one activity/usually forgets about it when interrupted	= Short attention span and low persistence

NOTES

[1] Raymond S. Moore, Ed.D., Martha Lorenz, Ph.D., Dennis Moore, Ingram F. duPreez, and T. Joseph Willey, M.D., "Influences on Learning in Early Childhood," manuscripts and synopsis available, Hewitt Research Foundation, University Station, Berrien Springs, Mich. 49104.

CHAPTER THREE

The First Three Years

Your daughter will grow and change at a phenomenal rate in her first years. By her third birthday she may weigh five times as much as she did when she was born. She will be twice as tall. She will have changed so much that you'll find it hard to remember how fragile, formless, even unreal she looked in her first days. She will walk, run, climb up stairs and onto furniture and counters to get what she wants. She'll jump down, hop, and skip. She may say whole sentences—short ones; she may even carry a simple tune. She'll know what everything and everyone around her is called. In fact, she'll probably be able to name familiar things from their pictures. She may surprise you by calling family friends by name after the first or second meeting, before her third birthday. But, almost more exciting to her parents, she'll be giving you very definite indications of the kind of person she's going to be.

Learning to sit, walk, talk, and remember is a natural

part of growing. But parents will have almost as much influence on her developing personality as her genes and chromosomes do.

In the first years the baby begins to form her impressions of grownups: Are people helpful or hurtful? Of herself: Am I nice? Can I get what I like and want and need?

Her parents are the mirrors in which she sees the answers. The way you touch your daughter and handle her; the way you behave around her; your response to her cries, smiles, protests, hugs, physical needs, will gradually help establish the way she sees herself and the world.

If you are observant and perceptive and get to know her well, and if you can treat her with respectful patience as you slowly persuade her to accommodate her ways to the family's routines and needs, you and she will probably be off to a happy start. Family life will be fun. Tension will be minimal. Your daughter will reflect this pleasant state of affairs. She'll be a comfortable part of a happy combination and she'll feel good. That comfortable confidence in herself and you will be money in the bank. When the inevitable problems develop later on, this solid foundation of early trust will make it easier to work them out together.

You can't help paying attention, even doting on your baby. Not everyone will necessarily share your enthusiasm. She's not theirs. They may *tell* you that your daughter is marvelous or exceptional. They may say that she is the most alert newborn they've ever seen. They may agree with you that her week-old smile is *real*, but they'll probably be thinking, "Another baby"; "They're all alike. Maybe at six months they're fun."

Of course, all babies are not alike, and even their minute differences are going to entrance their fathers and mothers.

Fathers—now that they've become parents, too—can be just as addicted to cataloguing the fine points of the baby's

28

individuality as mothers. Recently we heard a new father solemnly announce that the curl just above the opening in his daughter's ear was identical to his wife's, although the baby's ear *lobe* was shaped like his brother's.

Paying attention is easy, especially in the first weeks. Parents tend to pick up new babies at the slightest sniffle or sneeze. There are also endless hours of feeding, bubbling, rocking, and just holding in which to gaze, admire, and get acquainted.

While you're sizing your child up for looks and predicting her eventual height and shape, you will probably begin making a stab at assessing her temperament—although you may call it personality or character. Don't be too sure of your early judgments. Babies come on the scene a bit uncertainly, after all those months in the complete comfort and protection of the womb. They need time to settle down and get their bearings.

For nine months your baby has been nourished by the maternal blood stream, absorbing the nutrients and the oxygen necessary for life and growth through her umbilical cord. While she may have heaved a sigh or so for practice (her lungs were fully developed before she was born), and hiccuped occasionally (suggesting that something was going on in her digestive tract), leaving the watery haven of the womb is a drastic change. Now she has to make it all alone.

She has to learn to breathe efficiently. She has to learn to suck, digest, and eliminate satisfactorily and comfortably. The mechanisms that regulate body temperature may go through a shakedown period before they work smoothly. And many other body systems need a similar adjustment period. The infinitude of these adjustments explains the newborn baby's lability at this time. You'll notice that your daughter's breathing is rapid, shallow, and quite irregular. Her heart may beat so fast it frightens you. In the midst of a

29

quiet, peaceful sleep she will startle suddenly, as if a bomb had gone off in her bassinet. This unsettled state of affairs obviously affects behavior. Often babies are not steady at first. Their appetites, their sleep periods, their elimination, their comfort-discomfort range are all a bit uncertain. Therefore you can't go making cosmic predictions about them two days after you bring them home from the hospital. One child may seem as steady as Gibraltar one day and wake up at two-hour intervals, around the clock, the next. The next baby may be hard to get started nursing at each feeding and have trouble settling down to sleep afterward. She may be restless and fussy again soon after she drops off. Then, suddenly, at ten days or two weeks, she will sleep through the night, wake up ravenous, get hungry every four hours, and be a model of regularity ever after.

In these first weeks you won't be worrying about schedules and family routines. You'll be concentrating on making your daughter feel perfectly at home. You'll come when she calls. You won't make any effort to decide whether her cry means hunger, pain, or slow adaptability. This early behavior is not reliably predictive of her ultimate temperamental profile. However, the rank and file of newborns will certainly give you substantial clues to what they'll be like by the end of five weeks or two months.

By then, nine times out of ten, your baby girl will be following a pretty regular routine of eating, sleeping, crying, gazing into middle space. She will probably give you eight hours' sleep at night and you will be able to judge correctly that she is an "easy" baby, which most babies seem to be.

"Easy" babies are everybody's favorites. They have all the qualities of temperament that make parents' and later teachers' and friends' lives run smoothly. They get hungry at regular intervals, eat up without too much dallying, fall asleep promptly, sleep for predictable periods, and stay awake at predictable periods every day. They burp easily and seldom have gas pains that keep them awake. Their bowels move at the same times every day. If you try a new food, they may make a horrible face and shudder, but they usually end up opening their little mouths for more and eating up happily—at the second or third encounter, anyway. They smile easily. They're huggable. They don't stiffen up or push away when a stranger holds them. They like bathing.

Physiology may be the key. They fit in well because they seem to go along on a fairly even keel.

If you were taking care of a baby like that, wouldn't you like her, too? She makes the tiring part of parenthood as pleasant and unburdensome as possible. Meanwhile, she's making you think you're "natural" parents, very efficient at it all and very appreciated. So you're just bound to feed back smiles and praise and appreciation. That, in turn, stimulates her to even more of the same pleasing behavior. Most babies are like this, with minor variations. Getting along with them in the first years is almost automatic.

The "difficult" baby is the one who creates a challenge for her parents. Where the easy baby is regular in her habits, demands, and needs, the difficult baby is erratic. Her appetite is unstable. Her sleep is uneasy. Her reaction to everything you do, everything that happens, is intense and persistent. She is not easy to comfort or to please. It is hard to know what's wrong for the simple reason that she rarely lets you know when you've fixed it. In a nutshell, she will be irregular in her biological activity—hunger, fatigue, appetite, sleep, digestion. She will not adapt easily. She will be instinctively negative rather than positive about what goes on within and around her. She will be very intense in expressing herself and quite resistant to changing her first reactions to people and things.

We realize that, without a particular "difficult" baby for

you to observe as you read, she will sound alarmingly unappealing. It's all in how you approach her and what you do.

Fortunately you don't have to become a Marine Corps sergeant in the first years. Discipline—if that is not too stern a word at this stage—will be directed to helping your daughter adapt to the basic routines of life. The baby's needs are simple: enough food and sleep to satisfy, and enough conversation and comfort to give her the idea that she's welcome and that the world's worth exploring.

Gradually, if you are properly attentive to your baby's ways and her inner clock, she will adapt to the routines and rules you set for her in the interest of family welfare.

As we have said, family life revolves around the baby in her first weeks. Then, as she gets herself together and her responses become more stable, she can begin to accommodate her needs to you.

The "easy" baby will begin to sleep from her last evening feeding until 5 or 6 A.M. after the first weeks. She'll eat until full every time unless she's sick or upset. She'll fall asleep after burping, or sometimes even without. She'll wake up when she's hungry, and after a few weeks she'll wake up and *not* be hungry. She'll wake up to look at her hands or struggle to reach a bright-colored rattle hanging beside her in the bassinet or crib. She'll simply lie and stare at a bright color. Then she'll cry, quietly at first, and finally very insistently, expressing hunger and demand.

She'll love being bathed. She'll love being dried. She won't be too resistant to being dressed and diapered. By the time she is five or six months old she may even help you dress her by thrusting arms in armholes and putting her legs in the air when you change her diapers. If you put her to bed at ten she'll sleep just as well and as long as when you feed her and bed her down at midnight on evenings when you go out. She'll be happy with almost anyone for a sitter.

If you keep her up to sit with you when you have dinner, she'll be happy to listen and watch you without being held. If you prefer to put her to bed and eat by yourselves, she'll probably play quietly or fall asleep in her crib.

She will be just as adaptable *as you want her to be.* Therein lies the danger, *if any.* Her charming ways can be seductive. This is a big help at first, when you are getting acquainted and adjusting to her. When she begins to play wooing games, when she can talk, walk, and understand, her talent for sociability may distract you from your purpose now and then. This is the toddler who takes her animals to the toilet, when you thought you were taking her. You will listen, fascinated, as she toilet-trains them one after another, and forget to notice that she never trained herself—or even sat down.

Parents eventually want even the nicest baby to learn a few ground rules. In most households these focus around meals, baths, bedtime, and cleanup. Parents usually like to have dinner at a regular time. They like to have their evenings free for relaxation, whether they intend to stay home or go out. Around her first birthday, the baby starts to help feed herself and you think she might as well begin to do it with minimal mess and reasonable efficiency. Before you begin teaching—and this applies to any lesson, anywhere along—be sure you've decided what your goals are, and whether they're reasonable, given the child's age and particular abilities.

Let's say your daughter is fourteen months old. She's eating supper in her high chair. She's begun to drink from a cup by herself. She likes to feed herself. *But* she's just as likely as not to hold her cup over the edge and watch the milk pour out and the cat or dog run madly to lick it up. She's just as likely to feed her food to the dog as put it into her mouth. If there's no dog to give her ideas, she is perfectly happy simply pushing the food off the tray. No malice, you understand. She treats milk and oranges and gooey cereal and mashed fruit just the way she would finger paints or mud or sand and water at the seashore.

You want to teach her the difference. You will tell her with a simple "No" that what she's doing is wrong. But at her age it would be ridiculous to tell her why or expect her not to do it again. The game is irresistible. You don't want to take her food away. You want her to help herself. That's how she learns to do it right, eventually. So, if you don't like to clean up messes and replace her food, you must sit beside her, watch her every move, and intervene quickly and quietly when she shows signs of going primitive. Take the cup before she overturns it. Remove food if she starts to toss it.

You can, alternatively, let her practice self-feeding with something relatively baby-proof. Not a banana. She might want to squeeze it into a globby mush and paint with it. Better a piece of toast or cookie or apple. Take the food away only if she has lost interest in eating and is using it for play. In that way she begins to learn what food and meals are about.

If you want her to learn to manage her cup properly, teach her to ask for her milk when she wants to drink. Remove it between times. That way you can frustrate the impulse to pour if it overtakes her.

Now, not even the easiest babies will go right along with your best-laid plans every time. They want to get out of the high chair. They get tired of sitting in one position after a while. They want to play with the cat or see who made the noise outside or go to the bathroom. They can easily turn this back-and-forth business into a major daytime occupation.

You may decide on a rule or two here. (1) When you're

34

full, you're full. When you get down (except for emergencies like toileting), that's the end of that meal. (2) No games. If you have to go to the bathroom, go. Don't use it as an excuse for dawdling, or taking a detour to the blocks, or the train, or doll, or kitten.

Of course, you won't explain all this to a year-old daughter, or even a two-year-old. In fact, explaining too much is a common failing of conscientious parents. Bright and adaptable daughters are quick to exploit it. They listen to reasons and keep asking for more rather than conforming to requests.

Teaching a few rules and routines early is worthwhile. There is nothing more tiring for parents than children who dawdle, run back and forth from the table, knock over glasses, play with food. This kind of behavior makes the baby a constant center of distraction and causes the parents or helper unnecessary time and effort. Then weary impatience, rather than enjoyment, becomes the prevailing tone of family relations.

Set the rules but don't expect your daughter to conform like magic. Babies can't help getting restless, can't resist playing, can't help being clumsy.

The "easy" baby can outwit her parents just as easily as the "difficult" one. She is so charming that parents don't quite realize what's happening until it's all over (at least temporarily). When she gets down to go to the bathroom and comes back wanting her food fifteen minutes later, she'll probably have a present for the person who's attempting to bring her into line—a drawing she's crayoned, or one of her books, so you can read to her. You know the rule has been violated, but she's so sweet and pleasant and *resourceful*—all those qualities you admire—that you let her go back to her chicken and carrots and start to read to her. You finish the book to find she hasn't eaten a bite. You feed her a few mouthfuls. She wants the book again. She begins telling you the names of things in the pictures. She's stopped eating again. All very pleasant, but the results are nil. She has charmed you out of your purpose. You have taught her nothing.

The openly unco-operative child is more decisive and direct. She pours out the milk. When you take the cup away she screams, kicks, and wriggles until you think she'll fall out of her chair. When you give her the toast, *and* another chance, she throws the toast, still screaming. You want to take her down to enforce your rules about mealtime. But that means depriving her of a meal! Cruel treatment for one so young (a year to a year and a half) and, you fear, even bad for her health, though you know that one meal gained or lost won't stunt her growth or upset her nutritional balance.

You feel brave and decide to go through with your resolution to teach mealtime rules, so you take her out of her high chair and proceed to the next item on the agenda: nap time. This is hard. Daughter is not going to like it one bit. She may very well cry herself into hiccups—or, if she's just eaten, nausea. If she stops crying, she'll start demanding food in a very intelligible if wordless way.

Some parents relent . . . and relent and relent. Even when they're exhausted, the difficult child is dreaming up new and more impossible demands. When babies have no interior regularity, parents have to impose routines to help keep them together and at peace. Some parents have the intuitive wisdom or the instinctive inner need to start regulating their irregular babies calmly, coolly, and firmly very early. This takes a certain detachment plus the inner confidence to recognize that, no matter how cruel the weeping, protesting baby makes you feel, what you are doing is really best for all of you in the long run. Calm consistency will gradually accustom your daughter to the basic routines of family life. Then routines will not dominate the household and you will have time to enjoy your child's more appealing and positive qualities. Your enjoyment will make her happier and more eager to please and follow you.

If you let a difficult child call the shots, you will all be lost. We see this happen often. Instead of being in control, parents are guided by the child's chronic dissatisfaction. To satisfy the child, they abandon family routines and their own privacy, rest, and relaxation. The more they try to please, the less success they have. They assume that their irregular, sensitive, persistent, nonadaptive child knows what she wants and that they, her parents, are simply not sensitive enough to identify it. In fact, this child does *not* know what she wants. She is looking for direction and stability. When parents try to follow *her* cues, it only confuses her further.

There is another nonproductive result. Eventually the most patient parents reach the end of their rope. At this point, they will crack down suddenly and unexpectedly, and often with real anger. Anger and disapproval make things worse for the child. Even the most pleasant toddler's behavior deteriorates when she feels rejected. A vicious circle now begins. The parents feel guilty for their perfectly normal, if tardy, response. The child behaves worse. The parents try harder to appease, then crack down again. Sometimes this leads to disagreement and dissent between parents. They no longer work as a team. The child threatens their relationship.

This may sound discouraging. If it does, remember, only one little girl in a hundred is as hard to handle as the hypothetical one we've just described. And probably very few will be *quite* as peaches-and-creamy as the good little girl we call "easy." What you are more likely to find is a child with one or more behavioral traits that may create some present or future social or academic problem. Problems are bound to arise in the most idyllic circumstances, with the best parents and sweetest babies, but they don't have to get out of hand if you are attentive and alert to your daughter's behavior in the early years and learn to suit your reactions to her rhythms.

Of course, this means treating children differently. You could keep one baby up until ten one night, to suit your plans, and she'd settle right back to her 6 P.M. bedtime the next day. A less adaptable child might be up ten nights in a row if you changed her bedtime once. One child can be the enthusiastic center of a circle of indulgent relatives for a day-long family party and be perfectly happy playing alone the next day. Another might mope and cry for days after such an outing. Parents can carry some babies with them wherever they go, and bed them in strange places without a whimper of protest. They'll wake up out of a sound sleep, coo and play gaily all the way home, then close their eyes again the moment they are back in their own cribs.

Others will wake up when the phone rings, cry when they're wet or soiled, insist on a steady diet of bananas and nothing else for weeks on end, and howl when anyone but mother and father looks at them.

There are two ways of handling behavior that threatens to create an adjustment problem. One way is helpful, and one is harmful and counterproductive. If you recognize and accept your child's temperament, and make it your goal to help her modify and control it so that it does not get in her way or the family's, you set a constructive pattern for getting along. If you reject the behavior, as if it didn't exist, or act as if it were a nasty habit the child has developed to make life hard for you, you may create a behavior problem and a problem relationship with your daughter that will have far-reaching effects on personality development. Before she walks or talks, the child will begin to feel bad, flawed, uncomfortable with herself.

You can give the dawdler fair warning when something has to get done on time; then follow through firmly, despite protest, until she learns the lesson. Or you can get mad, plop her unceremoniously into the tub, put her to bed screaming and feeling abandoned and unlovable. Try to suit your tactics to her nature. You will preserve her pride and affection and they will help make the next lesson easier for her.

We hope that in trying to impress you with the significance of temperament we have not made you think that your daughter's distinctive behavior is the only, or even the most important, thing for you to consider. A child is more than the sum of her parts. So are you. What you feel about life, about each other, about being parents—if it's on the positive side—is probably transcendent. If you enjoy your daughter, enjoy the whims and fancies, funny quirks, blind spots, and special abilities that define her, and show a decent sensitivity to her needs from year to year, that will compensate for all the inevitable false moves and sins of commission and omission and have a dominant influence on your relationship.

Some people love little, little babies. Some people can't see a thing in them until they begin to smile and show signs of learning something. But when they struggle to their feet, totter alone, finally take their first steps and try to talk early in the second year, there's hardly a parent in the world who doesn't get excited.

Of course, these moves mark an enormous developmental milestone. Symbolically, being vertical is the beginning of independence. The child's perspective when she stands changes completely. From now on she is going to make her mark on the world. Her passive baby days are behind her. She can get around, and open doors and even drawers, knock things over, climb, fall, hurt herself, and break your possessions, and make messes. It's wonderful fun watching her watch herself in the mirror, figuring that other face out, kissing it, trying to hold it tight. It's marvelous how resourceful she is at taking every single object out of the kitchen cupboard, getting in and making herself a nest, then leaving it all for you to put back. She's fun. She's exhausting. What's more, she absolutely has to begin to learn what's what, what's whose, what's off bounds, and so on. You can take her temperament into account and accommodate yourself to her ways to perfection in an effort to get her to suit your civilizing strictures. It's still exhausting.

Hopefully you'll get some relief. Parents can relieve each other. There's the play group. There's day care. There's the sitter. Don't be afraid to get help when you need it, if you can. If you want it, you're going to find a way and you should. Baby care at best is not natural full-time business for most adults. Babies can't help you out by going off and reading a book for a few hours, no matter how inclined they are by temperament to want to please. They need almost constant supervision at this stage from enthusiastic, caring people. Of course, no baby ever gets as much dedicated, perceptive, affectionate, and—let's face it—*perfect* care as she'd like. Babies are megalomaniacs. They think they're the center of the universe. They have to be dissuaded. It's a bitter pill, but they can swallow it much better if they have understanding, encouragement, and love as they take their first steps away from you and begin to find that there are limits to their domain. To keep yourself patient, loving, and enthusiastic, get some help, if you need it, now.

Babies have some of the same ambivalence about their freedom that you may have. They want it, but they hate to pay the price. It's exciting. It's irresistible. The mountain (which may be the chair with the red car in its corner) is beckoning, because it's there. The baby tries to climb up on the chair. The chair falls on top of her as she makes her first try. Think of the courage it takes to try again.

The world is full of unknowns: dark corners of closets, roaring waterfalls in toilets, washers, dryers, Disposalls, vacuum cleaners roaring and swallowing everything in sight.

Babies want to be independent, but they want to be babies, too. They get very tired. They don't want to go to sleep and give up their full-time exploration. They fight bedtime. They fall. They protest. They want to feed themselves. They want to throw food, squash food, feed it to the dog. They want their independence. They don't want *you* to feed them. They won't open their mouths when you try.

They give you nightmares, sometimes, about survival. You are lost. You are falling. They give *themselves* nightmares, too. Maybe they're falling, too, or watching you fall, trying to catch you, watching you disappear.

Of course, we don't know what their dreams are. What we suspect, however, is that the unavoidable trauma of growing up, the vision of responsibility that babies must sense subliminally when they're one going on two, and the residue of tension from the encounters of daily life that they take to bed with them make them wake up frightened and scared. Independence, as always, is not quite as exciting and carefree as it appears.

This does not mean that your daughter is insecure or suffering because you've begun to leave her, more and more, or because you've been too demanding about civilizing her. It's because she's one going on two, and passing through an age of anxiety. Anxiety is normal. It is probably all that keeps any of us from getting into one long series of

41

exciting but foolhardy, if not fatal, encounters all through life.

If your daughter wakes up at night, steal quietly into her room and comfort her, silently, perhaps. Just rub her back a little, kiss, cover, pat, soothe. Often she won't even wake up completely. If she is really terrified, pick her up, put the light on, talk to her, and reassure her. Chase the bad dream world away with your real touch, the sight of her real surroundings. Give her a drink. Then turn off the light, put her back in her crib, and pat her for a few moments more before you go back to bed.

A bit of cautionary advice: it's tempting, when you're dead tired, and your daughter starts crying the moment you start to leave, to take her with you and tuck her into bed beside you. Don't start. You'll invite trouble for both of you. You don't really want a child in your bed. You want your sleep and your privacy. She needs to sleep, in private, too. Take the time now to comfort her until she goes to sleep. Or, if you're sure the fright is over, let her cry. You can leave the door open. You can leave the night light on. But leave.

A second word of caution: *nightly* nightmares of this intensity are something else. They may indeed reflect too strenuous daytime controls. It's worth reviewing the current parent-child and sitter-child relationships. It's not unusual to have several encounters a day with a one- to two-year-old without realizing how frequent they are becoming. They may also be getting a little rougher than they should be. Review things. Relax. If too much milk is going over the high-chair tray, for example, stirring up too many angry words and abrupt endings to meals, take away the cup or limit the contents to a swallow or two. Give up the toilet training temporarily if the sessions are tense. Get resourceful. Limit the areas of conflict. Lower your standards.

At the height of the laissez-faire era of child care, pediatricians would encourage you in your do-nothing attitude toward toilet training by reminding you that there's never been a college freshman in a diaper. The point is, socialization will happen, even without your unremitting twenty-four-hours-a-day vigil. Sometimes if you plant seeds too early in the spring they don't germinate as fast or grow as well as later plantings.

If you don't challenge your daughter's will to independence too severely and too suddenly, it will be easier for you both. It will also be easier to enjoy her, and thus easier to show approval, to pick up and hug and delight in your daughter, easily and often. Remember, she gets a good measure of her feelings about herself from your voice, your hands, and your face. She still reflects your attitudes. If you love her, she loves herself. If you approve, she approves. She's no different from you. When she feels she's okay, she acts okay, within the limits of her capacity.

A wise nursery school teacher, speaking of the importance of avoiding repressive encounters with very small children, said, "There is always another door to the house."

Of course you have to teach your child, for her health and safety, for family comfort, peace, and sanity, and in the interest of her own adaptation to the world. But there's lots of time. Almost nothing has to be done *now*. If you are in a hurry—and everyone is, from time to time—give up the bath rather than fight over it. Let her have the bowel movement in her pants, even if she knows better, rather than fight over staying on the toilet. Tomorrow is another day. Watch her, listen to her, remember who she is, where she is, and where you are trying to go, and you'll find the door that will lead there happily.

A word about liberating your baby girl. "What's new?" is a standard American greeting. Last year's toothpaste, coffee maker, even blue jeans and child care are not good enough. In the U.S.A., new is better, by definition. This leads us to faddish excess now and then. A few generations back, parents sterilized everything, almost including the baby, to guard against infection.

More recently, the mania for mental hygiene produced parallel excesses. Santa Claus was "out." It was feared that children, discovering the truth, would distrust their parents for ever after. Fairy tales were cleaned up: too fearsome! Children were not allowed to let their imaginations help them practice coping with their normal childhood fears.

Now we risk homogenizing the sexes in our proper concern for seeing that our girl children get the same chances at life as their brothers.

Not long ago some ingenious investigators devised a simple strategy to uncover mothers' hidden sex bias.[1] They gathered eleven young women, all of whom had small children of both sexes. The mothers, without exception, assured the investigators that they treated their boys and girls identically. They were then exposed, one at a time, to a six-month-old baby for a fifteen-minute play period. Six of the women had a baby dressed in blue, and introduced as a boy, to play with. Five had a baby dressed in pink and introduced as a girl. They all had three toys—a doll, a train, and a fish.

The five women with the girl *all* played with the doll. The six with the boy *all* played with the train; none of them offered their baby the doll. At the end of the play period each woman was asked to name any particularly masculine or feminine traits in the baby she had played with. All of them denied noticing any. However, when the women who had played with the "girl" were told that the baby, despite the pink outfit, was actually a boy, they refused to believe it.

This little exercise could be taken as certifiable evidence

that parents discriminate, willy-nilly, and interfere with their daughters' development from birth. Certainly our childhood experience and the culture we live in sometimes exert an influence that makes us act against our conscious purposes. Before we take our daughters out of their pink, however, it may be sensible to think about what we're after.

We can take away their dolls and give them trucks. We can restrain the impulse to encourage their first soft strands of hair to curl. We can dress them in sunsuits with lions and airplanes instead of birds and flowers. We can stop cooing and discourage fathers from showing pleasure in their daughters' femininity.

However, the purpose of liberation is to expand girls' range of expressiveness and give them more freedom to develop as they choose. Defeminizing them, treating them like boys, simply substitutes a new set of restrictions for the old ones. Being born female limits girls, today, only as we impose limits.

As soon as parents get too self-conscious about achieving goals with their babies, they start pushing and prodding them to conform. If you try too hard you will end up repressing instead of liberating. Don't forget they're only babies. They have to get their feet firmly on the ground and find their place in the world before they can worry about where they're going. Make them at home, enjoy them, let them be, control as needed, and as *un*repressively as you can, and—from all we know about how babies grow—you will encourage the energy, will, and confidence that will get them where they want to go, at the proper time. Take care of their *babyness* and they will probably liberate themselves.

SUGGESTED READING LIST

Brazelton, T. Berry, M.D. *Infants and Mothers.* New York: Delacorte, 1969; Dell paperback.

——. *Toddlers and Parents.* New York: Dell, 1974.

Briggs, Dorothy Corkille. *Your Child's Self-Esteem.* Garden City, N.Y.: Doubleday & Company, 1970; Doubleday paperback, 1975.

Chess, Stella, M.D.; Thomas, Alexander, M.D.; and Birch, Herbert, M.D. *Your Child Is a Person.* New York: Viking Press, 1965 (paperback).

Fraiberg, Selma. *The Magic Years.* New York: Scribner's, 1968; also paperback.

Gesell, Arnold, M.D. *The First Five Years of Life.* New York: Harper & Row, 1940.

Gesell, Arnold, M.D., and Ilg, Frances L., M.D. *Infant and Child in the Culture of Today.* New York: Harper & Row, 1943; rev. ed. 1974.

Murphy, Lois Barclay, and Associates. *The Widening World of Childhood.* New York: Basic Books, 1962.

Pomeranz, Virginia, M.D., with Schultz, Dodi. *The First Five Years.* Garden City, N.Y.: Doubleday & Company, 1973; Dell paperback, 1976.

NOTES

[1] Jerrie Ann Will, Patricia A. Self, and Nancy Datan, "Maternal Behavior and Perceived Sex of Infant," *American Journal of Orthopsychiatry,* Vol. 46, No. 1 (January 1976), p. 135.

CHAPTER FOUR

The Nursery Years

Three to Five

The three-year-old copycat is beginning to have taste, style, interests, social sense, and a mind of her own by the time she is five. She is strongly hinting at the person she will be.

Her leaps and bounds in mental and emotional development during these years are as dramatic as the spurt in her physical growth from birth to three.

When your three-year-old draws a mommy or daddy, it's a lopsided circle—maybe not even quite joined.

When your five-year-old draws a person, you can't mistake it. It has head, arms, legs, a body of sorts, most of the correct features, and, occasionally, clothes and ten fingers and toes, which the artist will painfully count out while drawing. The person has not only a sex ("Don't you see the hair?" or "the lipstick?") but feelings. The person is smiling along with the sun in happy pictures. In sad pictures, rain sometimes falls and people wear turned-down mouths.

Five-year-olds can see and reproduce the difference be-

47

tween the letters *O* and *G,* and *D* and *Q*—putting the straight parts and the open parts and the distinctive slash of the *Q* in the proper places. They can make an *I* and turn it into a *T, J,* or *L,* and they usually know that we write from left to right, even if they don't always do it.

Fine-finger-muscle development accounts for this progress only partially. Hand-eye co-ordination has become more sophisticated, and so have perceptions. At five, a girl is simply more aware in all ways. Suddenly all the things she has been seeing, copying, forgetting, trying again; all the things she has been watching with no apparent reaction; all the things you have been showing and telling; indeed, the sum total of her experience since birth, seem to fall into place in her mind. From being naïve and fragmentary, her understanding begins to be comprehensive and mature.

She is starting to be really at home in her world by five.

She has developed taste of her own: in clothes, colors, foods, fun. A three-year-old will let *you* do the dressing. If she's interested at all, it will be in showing how much she can do by herself or insisting on wearing her favorite *red* shoes or *soft* sweater or her fancy *party* dress.

At five she'll know what she likes. She is beginning to worry about what's proper, even if she's not sure what is. She's trying intermittently to be independent. A five-year-old we know was going to cross the country alone with her father to visit her grandmother. She insisted that her mother put a note in her suitcase listing what to wear with what because "Daddy doesn't know those things." Five-year-olds of both sexes have begun to have opinions not only about what they like to wear but about flavors, smells, and sounds.

This is the age when children who have had a chance to experiment and explore will be developing passions: for artichokes; for a subtly blended salad dressing; for a particular fluffy, squunchy, tart dessert; for lemons. They're beginning to appreciate textures—the feeling of, the looks of things. As they explore and discover, their judgments grow bolder. Expressing them seems to be essential to making them their own.

"Yuck!" a five-year-old will say. "What a smell!" Or "I hate that color—take it away." Or "Gross"—borrowed probably from an older sister or brother.

Growing sophistication extends to words and word play. Fives give modest evidence of burgeoning wit in their addiction to riddles, for example.

"What's the difference between an egg and an elephant?" a five-year-old will ask, dancing up and down and begging you to give up. And when, as inevitably happens, you do, she'll collapse in spasms of giggles. "Well, if you don't know the difference between an egg and an elephant, I guess I can't send *you* for groceries."

She's beginning to sort out people along with things. As she begins to figure out how her world works, she develops self-awareness and becomes a little less subjective. Everything and everyone does not always have to revolve around her. There's room for other people now.

A young camp counselor making the midnight rounds heard someone sobbing in the seven-year cabin. She started to go in when she heard a child's voice: "Don't cry. I know your mommy and daddy are thinking about you right now. You know what, I bet they're sitting there writing to you this very minute. Pretty soon you're going to get a letter from them—maybe tomorrow. We can play jacks after breakfast. You like that. Okay?"

It was the youngest child in camp—just five—comforting her bunkmate—almost seven. Sure enough, the sobbing stopped.

The five-year-old can put herself in the other child's body, feel her feelings, *empathize*. This new talent reflects her rapidly developing awareness of the social scene. She is learning to anticipate the responses and reactions of people around her and adapt her own behavior accordingly. She knows better than to kick the seat in front on a public bus, be rude to strangers, or attract attention by misbehaving in public. She won't tell her friend's mother she hates ice cream with bumps in it even though she can't quite bring herself to eat the stuff.

Her social sense and self-awareness develop hand in hand. She suddenly seems to have absorbed enough from observation and experience to make the incredible mental leap that allows her to generalize.

She sometimes, in fact, *seems* quite grown-up, but she isn't. That's why you may find her sobbing as if abandoned for good when you're ten minutes late to pick her up at school. In fact, an uneasy mixture of social sophistication and anxious dependence characterizes her behavior as she explores, investigates, and tests both in play and in her dealings with her parents and others. She is constantly trying to figure out who she is, where she belongs, what's expected, what she can and cannot do, whether she's safe. All this helps her define herself, her place in the family, and her role in everyday life, and get at least a tentative idea of where she is headed.

Rules and controls give her orderly paths to guide her behavior until she is experienced, understanding, and strong enough to guide herself. Play gives her endless opportunity to try out all her ideas, wishes, and imaginings and judge them for herself. Play gives her a chance to test herself in freedom. She needs this experience in independence just as she needs grown-up guidance and secure controls to help her learn rules, routines, and limits for behavior in the family.

A friend visits for dinner. She brings four-year-old Harriet a coloring book of illustrations from *Peter Rabbit*. Harriet recognizes what they are immediately, hugs her friend warmly, plops down cozily in the family circle, and gets to work.

She makes Peter's coat red—almost any four-year-old's favorite color. "Oh no," Mother says helpfully. "What color is Peter's coat? Peter's coat is blue." She even goes and gets the book to prove it. Meanwhile Harriet is putting blue over red obediently and looking unhappy.

"It's all spoiled now. It's messy," she says.

Father tries to help. "Well," he says judiciously, "forget that picture. There are lots more."

Enthusiasm revives briefly. She begins to color the cabbage patch. "Careful, now," Mommy says. "Stay inside the lines."

Harriet tries to oblige because she's a very agreeable child, but her parents have missed the boat. At four, when she's trying so hard to find her place in the world and fit into it, it's more important than it is at almost any other age for her to have a chance in play to use her eyes, her ears, her hands and voice, her ideas, and her imagination without the slightest worry about how it all turns out, about success or failure, right or wrong, grownups' way versus hers. That's how she develops taste, knows what she likes to do and what bores her, and learns much more about herself, as you will see below.

Oddly enough, parents who may impose their grown-up ideas on children's play without thinking twice are sometimes hesitant about teaching their children the routines, behavior, rules, and limits that they need to learn to get along easily in the world.

Children at this age are learning so much, so constantly, and trying so hard that they make fascinating company. But there is a darker side.

Remember Memory, the game where you spread a pack of cards out upside down and try to turn up pairs? It's a favorite game for fours, fives, and some threes. But at every turn, over and over, the average child will pick up the very same card that she turned up first before. You may try to explain how turning up a fresh card first next time will increase her chances of making a pair, but it will be futile. She's not stupid, perverse, or stubborn. She's just learning at her age rate, and at three, four, or five it takes lots and lots of experience for anything new to be assimilated. You recognize this truth in Memory.

When it comes to daily life with daughter, it's not quite as much fun to watch.

"Why do I have to have a bath now?"

"Why can't I put my toys away later?"

"Why can't I play some more?"

"Why can't I have one more drink?"

"Why can't I come downstairs until you sit down for dinner?"

"If I just play here, why can't I stay up while you eat?"

"Why can't you read one more story? Just a short one?"

And so on, and so on.

Three to fives use the same repetitive technique they use in Memory to learn the rules, how much you'll give, what things mean, how strong they are vis-à-vis a grownup.

The same old questions, again and again, the whining, the begging, the wheedling, the resistance to following a routine, make you tired. If you're already tired, they make you impatient, cross. You don't want to be cross with such a little kid, because you know very well she needs your unswerving, affectionate devotion, so instead of stopping to figure out what the wheedling, dawdling, or whys are all about and responding appropriately, you try to be patient and sweet and explain and explain. Finally, maybe, you explode and assert your superior force.

It's easier, and more effective perhaps, to think before you react—not just about what your daughter is doing and why, but also about what you want her to learn.

Let's take questions.

Jeanie has just noticed sunlight reflecting on windows across the street. She asks if it is a fire. You tell her it's sun on the windows. She asks, "How can the sun be in the window when it's in the sky?"

Grandmother is entranced. "I've never heard such penetrating questions from a three-year-old."

Well, it goes on that way and you get to the point where you would trade her in for a really dumb kid who just asks things like "Why do I have to go to bed?"

But watch it, your three-year-old will ask that too.

There's the nub of the problem. A child at this age asks, asks, asks.

1. *She asks to find out* and she deserves as much respectful attention and as many clear, simple explanations as you can give. Telling too much confuses.

Take a favorite question: "How does the baby get out of Mommy's tummy?"

Don't go into a whole Masters and Johnson bit. Stick to the simplest answer. Talk in images a child can understand from her own experience. "The baby is in a kind of muscle bag. When it's ready to come out, the muscle squeezes. That makes the mother feel like pushing. It's a little like when you have a bowel movement. Mothers have a special opening for the baby to come out. As the muscle squeezes and the mommy pushes, the baby's head presses against the opening and finally it opens enough for the baby to get through." That's it.

2. *She asks because she's practicing words, learning the language.*

For example: "Why do you call Grandmother every day?" a little child might ask.

A four-year-old understands the answer right away. "I want to say hello. I want to find out how she is."

But she asks the next day because:

3. *She asks to try to find out something about life and herself.* She wants to understand your relationship to your mother, yours to her. She's trying to understand love and devotion, though she could never put that thought into words. She may want to know that *she* won't be forgotten by you when you leave *her* alone. So this is a question you answer again and again. And, if you think you know what's behind it, you might pull her up on your lap as you talk and hold her tight while you tell her, "I call because I love her, just as I love you. I like to hear her voice. I want to be close. I don't want her to think I've forgotten her. Do you love me too?"

4. *She also asks questions because she's learned that they get your attention,* postpone unpleasant events, and so on.

Marianne doesn't really like it when her lively Aunt Lisa comes—unless adored Aunt Lisa is playing with *her*. She keeps interrupting Lisa's effort to tell her mommy the last chapter in her job hunt.

"Why did the man ask you if you were going to get married?"

"Why is that bird eating so much bird seed?"

"Why didn't kitty drink his milk?"

"Mommy, why did Daddy leave his coffee in the cup?"

"Mommy, why don't you take the dishes off the table?"

"Daddy, don't you have to get the train?"

This is filibustering. Marianne is not asking for answers. She's asking for attention. She needs to know that *you* know what she's up to. Don't answer. Teach her that there are times and places when other people or business come first: for example, friends you are entertaining, your work, your rest, getting to bed, dressing for nursery school, and so on.

If nonstop questioning persists whenever your daughter does not have your undivided attention, it may mean that her need is temporarily greater than her ability to learn the lesson. Have you been gone all day? Have you been working hard evenings, too? Have you been rushing her through her morning time with her parents to be sure that she'll be ready to go off the moment the baby-sitter comes for her? Have either or both of her parents been more than normally concerned about a friend, a family problem, a career decision, taxes?

In short, is Marianne feeling squeezed? Are the questions a four-year-old effort to get a little of the mommy and poppy love she's missing?

There's a quick way to see. Drop whatever it is you're doing or saying for a few minutes. If you're rushing to get out, talking to a friend or spouse, excuse yourself. If you can't stop now, take the first opportunity to give your daughter all your attention, lovingly and unhurriedly. You may think you're much too busy, harassed. But the time spent will be time saved.

Answer the question—whatever the last one was—as simply as possible. Pick up your daughter and just enjoy her being for a moment. Then show her you think you know her game, in a humorous way, of course.

"Now, Marianne, why are you asking all these silly questions? What do you *really* want—a hug [give it], a story, a game, a little cuddling? How about five whole minutes—just you and me—like this? But no more silly questions for an hour—Okay?"

If it works for an hour or a half hour, increase the attention for a few days and see if the questions, or whatever other attention-getting device your daughter is using, slow down. You will teach her that making a nuisance of herself is *not* the way to get what she needs. You will teach her how to ask directly for what she wants.

5. *She may be asking questions to see how far you will go before you crack down* and make her eat her lunch, or forget it, undress and get into bed.

How can you tell? Looking back, remember the times and the circumstances when the barrage of questions took place. Does she use other ploys to achieve the same end? Wheedling—"Please let me"; "Just this once"; "I'm thirsty" —when she's supposed to go to bed and stay there. Or, "I have to get the tower on the house." Or, "You didn't read me *Curious George*," when she's asked you for quite a different book. "You have to read *Curious George*. You said you would last night."

Face these stalls just as matter-of-factly, humorously, and affectionately as if she were once more picking up that same old card in Memory. After all, it's just a different version of the learning game that includes testing, asking, seeing what happens.

Suppose it's a matter of getting out of her clothes so you can give her a bath. She has been told to stop playing and do it. Now she is still playing. You tell her again. She begins with the questions. "Why does rain make noise on the roof?" "What will we have for lunch when Billy comes?" "Are we going to visit Grandma on Sunday?" "Why do my feet smell?"

Don't answer at all. Ask, "Do you want to take your

clothes off or shall I do it for you?" It's best if you know she wants to do it herself but it's okay, anyway. If there's one more stall, one more question, you do the undressing. Sometimes action speaks louder than words, as the old saw goes. If you talk too much, a three-to-fiver may begin to think talking can keep anything at all she doesn't like from happening.

You will teach your daughter two important lessons. (1) Questions are serious efforts to get real information or help. You don't misuse questions or your parents' time and attention by asking them for phony reasons. (2) You had better know that there are play times, fun times, and times to do what you're told. This is a time to do what you're told. Just as Mommy and Daddy have to get to work on time, or be ready when dinner guests come or when the movie starts, you have to get to bed when we say and do whatever else we expect when the time comes—no kidding, no stalling.

Remember what the three-to-fiver is about. She's trying to figure out the system—*not to beat it*—at first. If there were only one rule in your house, she'd have to avoid it, get around it, make you forget it, in order to measure it, and learn from your firm and consistent reaction that it's a rule.

A granddaughter came to visit. We called her from the swing for lunch. She went on swinging. We called her twice. She asked us to push her. We called her three times. She wanted to know who put up the swing. We said, "What's the matter, Laurie, don't you come to lunch at your house when lunch is ready?" Her answer: "Yes, Grandma, Mommy calls me three times. Daddy calls me once. I wanted to see how many times you call."

TESTING, TESTING, TESTING IS THE NAME OF THE GAME: Finding out what the rules are; whether they're real; just how far parents bend and when they crack down. The method at the moment may be Why? Why? Why? But it may just as easily be straight evasion, nagging, whining, begging, or finally the divide-and-rule strategy.

Your matching tactics should be steady and unwavering —an achievement made much easier if you bear in mind that you are the parent and your child is the child. You are the teacher. She wants to learn. She is experimenting, exploring, testing, *to learn*. She is not trying to distract, delay, evade to unnerve or upset you.

Teach that no means no, that nagging doesn't work, that if Daddy says no, Mommy will say no too, and that if Mommy says no, there's no use asking Daddy.

You are not perfect. Sometimes you're tired, sometimes your child is tired or upset. Sometimes you're just too comfortable with your dinner guests to put your little girl back to bed and suffer through the crying she uses to test you. It won't be fatal. Don't be too ambitious in your goals. Set limits and rules you *can* enforce. Then be as consistent as you can about frustrating all efforts to evade, avoid, limit, or eliminate them.

These early social years when your daughter is still finding her place in the family and figuring out how the small world around her works and how to get into it, she is also getting her first notions of what it is to be a girl. Remember, however, that she is still fairly "primitive." She learns by watching, exploring, testing. She will notice before or about when she's three, depending on her experience, that boys have penises and girls don't. She may practice peeing standing up. She may start exploring her vagina in search of a penis or simply to see what's there. She may start exploring her playmate's penis. She's interested in learning through feeling. We doubt that her lack of penis makes her feel bereft or deprived. In our opinion, girls don't usually feel that way unless they've been made to.

The three- to five-year-old is not only curious, but sensual. She is almost certain to discover that masturbating feels good, and to indulge herself when there's nothing more important to do, or she feels like feeling better. It won't hurt her, will it? Don't interfere. If you say, "No! Naughty," or look cross and pull her hand away, she's going to *feel* naughty. She will go on masturbating secretly, because it is irresistible, apparently, at this stage, but she'll *feel* naughty and guilty and unworthy. This is most likely the origin of some girls' feelings of inferiority.

It is a good idea to let her know that masturbation is a private matter. If you don't, someone else—a teacher or a baby-sitter or a relative—will. People still frighten children about the evils or dangers of masturbating. Avoid that risk. If she masturbates in the living room, or in the grocery store or park, call her aside and give her a brief lesson about privacy. You give her lessons like this all the time—about eating with her hands, picking her nose in public, saying thank you, perhaps. You might say, "People don't handle their genitals in public. It isn't polite." No big deal. At this age, children are so busy learning to fit in that they quickly take the cues that grownups give them.

Their preoccupation with learning the rules, figuring out how the system is set up, makes them ultraconventional in some respects. They go for stereotypes. Thus four- and five-year-olds' play is permeated with the rankest sexism. No matter what their parents do and say, they play their mom and pop roles in ultraconventional style. We've seen little girls whose mothers are doctors absolutely refuse to take doctors' parts in their play, insisting that "only boys can be doctors," against all reason. Girls do more washing and drying of clothes, dishes, and babies than they've ever seen their own mothers do, and they turn their play husbands into TV-watching drones who do nothing but talk about money. This may make you edgy. You may try hard to persuade your little mother to be a working mommy—a doctor, an engineer, or a fire fighter, or whatever. You may push her to change husbands for a more congenial, co-operative, and housekeeping type. Don't interfere. Child's play is sacred business, almost. Butting in, directing it, is like butting into a child's fantasies, rewriting her first stories. It puts her down. It makes a child self-conscious about thoughts that must be free to be useful to her. It deprives her of the precious tool (her imagination) that will serve her in all sorts of creative ways through life.

The stereotyped roles a child plays serve all kinds of general developmental needs as well as the child's particular needs of the moment. Before a little girl can begin to establish her own identity, she has to find a category, a pigeonhole where she fits, just as she has to learn absolute rules before she can gain the sophistication to make exceptions. After she's played the mommy in conventional, ritualistic fashion, she can play around with ways to be her particular person and find her own brand of femininity.

Play also helps children cope with feelings. This is a time when children typically acquire baby brothers and sisters. A first child may be inflicted with a first sibling. A second child may lose her enviable spot and slip into that ambiguous in-between slot. It's unnerving, often. Just as they are beginning to be pretty sure of themselves, pretty proud of how they can stay clean and dry, put out the light when they go to bed, and walk into school without so much as a backward glance at Mommy or Daddy, this has to happen. Their world is upside down.

A new baby's mere presence stimulates an older child's anxiety about her place in the family. This uneasiness is constantly aggravated by the fact that new babies absorb so much of their parents' time. Of course, new babies are also exciting, mysterious, and full of fun and surprises for big brothers and sisters. They have some of the same fascination that kittens and puppies—those live, warm, wiggly, furry things—have for children. But siblings are first, last, and always a *problem*. So, naturally, little girls and little boys endlessly explore, test, experience, deal with what new babies do to their lives, through doll play.

Listen to the doll play and you will find out exactly what your little girl is taking in from you about what daddies do, what mommies do, what you expect of her as a person and what she is learning from you about being a girl.

Sarah and her friend, Tommy, are playing house. Tommy makes the doll child say, "Throw that baby out the attic window. He wets too much." Sarah talks for the mommy doll. "Oh no, dear, that's what babies do. You're big now. You don't have to cry like that. You help Mommy." Now Tommy is the daddy doll. "Before you know it, the baby will be someone for you to play with. You can teach him to talk."

They get a tub of water and plunk the baby in. "Drown him, drown him," Tom makes the doll child say. Sarah grabs the baby. "No, no. He's a nice little baby. He has feelings just like you." The boy doll (Tommy) says, "He cries too much." The mother says, "He must have pains. Burp him, Daddy." The daddy doll takes the baby tenderly and burps him. "Look, Mommy, he looks like Sarah. He's going to be beautiful." The mommy doll says, "Let's keep him, shall we?" She wraps the baby up, puts him in the bassinet, and pats him gently.

Children practice comforting, feeling, sympathizing with, caring for, and getting along with their dolls. They can express their jealousy, rejection, and rage harmlessly. They learn how to deal with their "bad" feelings. They figure out acceptable explanations for things that trouble them. They practice the way they want to be and the way you want them to be.

The birth of a baby rival is as hard on boys as on girls. All children have to figure out how to adjust to this dislocation, how to feel secure again with the rival, how to integrate their love and their hate, their rage and their tender feelings. In doll play, they experiment with, test out, and finally discover their own ways to cope.

In some circles, dolls are in disrepute, accused of perpetuating sexism, keeping girls in their place. Not so. In doll play, boys and girls together practice how to live, how to get along, how to express themselves and their feelings, how to love, care for, protect, be dependent. They try out *what* they want to be, *how* they want to be. They get their ideas from copying their parents and other important adults, and play them out until they are their own. If mothering and caring in your house are for women only and men have other work that is superior and important, that's how they'll play it. If you show them how to be capable and caring, how to work together instead of competing against; if you love and cherish, so will they—boys and girls together. They'll let their imaginations, through their dolls and their play, help them, at this very first stage of true social awareness, feel their way toward the kind of human beings they will be. Doll play isn't "masculine" or "feminine." Caring is human.

Q. Last week our children were playing in my daughter's bedroom. My friend was telling me about her sister who nearly bled to death when her baby was born. The baby died. The mother is still in the hospital and severely depressed. At one point in the story I noticed my little girl standing in the doorway looking absolutely desolate. When I asked her what was wrong she shook her head and ran back to play. I am afraid she heard our discussion. Will it hurt her?

A. It certainly could. Parents who wouldn't think of discussing financial problems before children sometimes forget that three-year-olds have ears when they are talking about the normal and abnormal events of pregnancy and childbirth. Children, as always, react differently to tales like this one. Your daughter gave a clear cue that she was quite frightened, while her friend, as far as you could see, remained oblivious. Outward appearance, however, is not always a reliable measure of what's going on inside. Girls may develop damaging fears about themselves, their bodies, and their prospects in life as women from hearing about the dangers and risks of motherhood and seeing the pain and suffering it causes. Clearly some children are more easily affected than others. Some are more sensitive by nature. Some are conditioned to be more sensitive by their own unhappiness and the unhappiness they feel in their mothers. Their childhood view of woman's lot doesn't excite them about their prospects. In any case, it is ill advised, in our opinion, to talk in front of children about operations, caesareans, placenta praevia, hemorrhaging, stitches, and grue-some details of childbirth.

Remember, in the preschool and early school years, fantasy and fact are very much intertwined in children's minds. Children develop theories about where babies come from and how they get started when they're as young as three. Some think the baby is born through the navel and that the mother explodes if she is not cut open in time. Some think babies come out of the rectum. Even when children get the point of exit correctly, the image of babies coming out of an opening as small as their own vagina can seem a pretty frightening prospect. Children of this age constantly add to and embroider each other's stock of myths and misconceptions.

At puberty, early fears and feelings associated with childhood fantasies are reactivated. Kiss and you get pregnant; you can get pregnant from a toilet seat; bad thoughts or masturbation can give you abnormal children; and so on. And once more, friends, educated in fallacies and all trying to top one another, fan the fears.

At puberty, girls are unusually preoccupied with themselves, their social position, and their abilities. They worry about development: Am I ever going to get breasts? Isn't my left breast much bigger than my right? Am I deformed? Do I have cancer? Will all my friends leave me for boy friends because I haven't had my period? Will that dream I had with all those feelings mean I'm going to be a nymphomaniac? Am I abnormal? . . .

If a girl has a comfortable, easy relationship with her parents and has been accustomed to asking them about things that trouble or puzzle her without fear of criticism or ridicule, she will ask questions as they come to her. She clears up her distorted ideas and comes out with a benign view of herself, as is, and her future as a woman.

However, all sorts of perfectly natural situations and events can prevent this happy development. Mothers can be unhappy or absent. Children can be temporarily on the outs with parents. Parents may not be able to communicate easily on sex or any other intimate subject. The child may have totally unrelated problems that make her more anxious than her friends. Then the normal concerns and questions about sex and being a woman assume undue importance. The fears and fantasies of early childhood don't go away. They may become obsessive. Guilt and fear build up and can create problems that interfere with development and achievement and satisfaction in adult life.

While a child is not going to become neurotic simply because she hears about childbirth or sees menstrual blood when she's very young, we feel it is unnecessary and insensitive to risk fueling the primitive imagination of the little girl with graphic details of the hazards that she may suffer as a woman.

CHAPTER FIVE

Out of the Home, into the World

Six to Eight

Life begins at six—at least in the minds of six-year-olds. These days, many college students don't bother to attend the graduation ceremony that marks their symbolic readiness for life. But starting first grade has not lost its glamour for six-year-olds. It may be the most important commencement in life.

In kindergarten you *are* the baby. In first grade you *put down* the baby. The first grade child graduates from infancy and starts out on her own. Independence at six may not seem quite total to parents and teachers, but to six-year-olds it is enormous.

First graders have *whole* books. They get *harder* and *longer*. Besides, there are *real* numbers to learn, and right and wrong answers. Every first grader knows in some osmotic way that this is real life. This is learning to be like Mommy and Daddy—big, responsible people who work and take care of small children. First grade is the first step on the way to a place in the grown-up world.

First grade is also the first time a girl is on her own with her peers. Kindergartners' mommies or daddies take them to school or come and get them. In most communities, first graders can come and go by themselves. Even in big cities or tiny villages where it's too dangerous or too far for them to come and go alone, they're on their own in school in a way kindergartners, cloistered in their classroom with their teachers, never know. They have to walk the halls with other children, go to the playground and the lunchroom on their own. No mommy or daddy to shield them, no teacher's watchful eye to spot the signs of trouble and intervene. Nobody to find friends or save them from their enemies. Being on the edge of independence for the first time is exhilarating, but it's also precarious.

First grade creates the same mixture of anticipatory excitement and fear in parents. Parents can't wait to see their daughter step out into the world. They're as eager for her reactions as they were when she took her first steps and said her first words. At the same time, there's a bit of anxiety. *How* will she do? How quickly will she learn? How will she compare with her classmates? What will the teacher think of her? How will she get along? Will she be a leader? Will she be able to find a secure place with her peers? Will she be happy? Will she achieve? How should I help her?

The fact that school is the child's initiation into the world where she will spend her life makes academic and social performance in the school setting the principal focus of parents' interest and concern during the early elementary years from six to eight.

The child copes with the anxiety that her new situation creates for her by bending every effort to find her niche in the new, uncharted land. She may turn her back, ceremoniously, on her former friends and protectors (you) and try to fit in. No matter who her parents are and how devoted

6 8

she has been, your six-year-old knows instinctively that, from now on, she has to learn to make her way with her peers, alone. The main thing on her mind is learning how to be a success.

Will I read as well as Marjorie? Will I read as well as Teacher wants me to? Will I make the numbers right? Does the seven go this way: 7—or this way: ⅁? Is this a D, or is it like this, ⅁? Is this way a Q, or this G? Now Dorothy is on number 3 pre-primer and I'm still on number 2 and Dorothy won't play with me any more because she's faster. Besides, she has a red dress and mine is green. I need a red dress. I like baseball but Dorothy says girls shouldn't play boys' games. I can't read out loud because everyone will see that I can't read as well as Dorothy.

Of course, this soliloquy is ours. We can't guarantee that it reproduces six-year-old thoughts and feelings exactly. But we have been there, and we have listened a good deal to what six-year-olds *say* goes through their minds. And since you have been there, too, you will remember, if you try, that it's very important to be good at whatever it is you are supposed to be in your first great new independent year—to do it all right.

All the changes and transformations, all the distinctively six-year-old behavior—or a great deal of it—stem from this central need, the need to fit.

Sevens and eights won't react as dramatically as six-year-old first graders. Exposure, experience, and the sophistication that age and time produce make them better able to cope with the vicissitudes of daily life—the challenges, the conflicts, the setbacks and disappointments. Nevertheless, measuring themselves against their peers, keeping track of how their elders are measuring *them,* and hanging in continue to occupy a major part of their minds and remain a major influence on their behavior during this period of development.

You may be horrified at what happens. For six years you have been learning her ways and adapting to them. For six years she has been learning yours. With a little help here and a little pressure there (tempered with love), she has adapted, too. Then a few weeks of first grade and *pfft!*—it's as if you dreamed it all.

Remember she's six. Remember what sixes have on their minds. It will keep you from doing too much too soon, a common but invariably unproductive practice of parents. There are times, and there always will be, when your children need your help. Age six, for your daughter, may be one of them. But the less obvious the help is to you or anyone else involved, the more it will help. Try to let your daughter master her tasks as she comes to them by herself. Independent success at this job will make the next challenge easier for her.

Let's take a hypothetical little girl, whom we'll call Joan, and see what might happen to her with four different kinds of parents.

Joan is a solid, patient, hard-working, careful child who does everything slowly, methodically, *and* successfully. She is off to a good start in first grade, except her best friend is the best reader, the fastest learner, and Joan begins to worry about keeping up.

Normally cheery and equable, she now becomes whiny. She teases her little brother. The carefully taught little girl, so calm, confident, industrious, and efficient in work and play, is falling apart.

Her mother, Mrs. P., panics. She and Mr. P. confer. They decide the system is to blame. They go to school and ask for extra reading help. They tell the teacher she's put-

70

ting on too much pressure. They accuse her of offering too much, too fast, and encouraging children to compete instead of fostering *real* values.

The teacher is alienated. Special reading help separates Joan from her friend and labels her a problem in the class when she isn't.

Mother and Father couldn't bear to "let Joan do it." For the first time in Joan's life, maybe, they forgot to deal with her as an individual. They forgot she had to learn her own way. They tried to change the school to suit her. It didn't work. In fact, their criticism of her teacher and the system Joan was trying hard to adapt to made her lose her bearings.

The second set of parents, the Q.'s, pretend Joan's problem doesn't exist. They tell Joan she is reading well enough to suit *them*—forgetting that they aren't the ones to set the standards. They give her extra understanding and LOVE. They know she is teasing her little brother because she is insecure. They don't tell her to stop, but say, "That's not kind. It hurts." They reassure her that a sweet child like her will always have friends.

Joan continues to tease her brother. She won't pick up her toys at bedtime. She won't dress herself any more. She cries when it is time to go to school.

Mr. and Mrs. Q. would have helped Joan more if they had ignored her completely. She didn't need their expressions of approval and offers of love. She knew they loved her. What she wanted was the badges of first grade success. She wanted to be as good a reader as her best friend. She wanted to be like the rest. Her social and academic status was very important to her. Putting down her first grade values didn't make them less important. It simply didn't help her.

The third hypothetical set of parents, the R.'s, blame Joan for her problems. They drill her at home until she cries with frustration and fatigue. They insist she can be best if she tries. Being first, in their minds, is the only way out of the dilemma. Since Joan can never be first, she is headed for sure disaster.

For one reason or another, Mr. and Mrs. T., the fourth set of parents, take their time. Maybe they are slow and patient like Joan. They watch and wait a bit. Then Mr. T. has a talk with the teacher on the phone. He finds Joan is getting along very well. He learns from the teacher that many of the children will gravitate to one "star" child at the start of the first grade but, as the year goes on, they almost all find more truly compatible friends and a place of their own.

"Don't worry too much, Mr. T. First grade is a big step, you know. I'll keep you posted." The teacher winds up cheerily and Mr. and Mrs. T. relax and begin to help Joan relax.

Being studious and methodical, Joan wants to have her parents help her at home. The teacher gives her little drills, which they go over with her at bedtime, before her story. Neither mother nor father tries to rev her up or put down the teacher, the class, or her ambitions. They just go right along as they always have. They listen and help her work toward her goals. At the same time they reassure her often that they agree with her teacher that she is moving fast enough.

They don't try to talk her out of her attachment to the number one reader. They do, however, encourage her to ask other children whom the teacher reports Joan likes to do things with them on weekends. Gradually the number one reader fades in importance. Joan settles down to working at her own pace, carefully and happily. By grade two she is perfectly comfortable and confident, both socially and academically.

First graders react the way we all do when we're alone in new situations. Some take a quick look at the new territory and engage in an immediate, massive, almost mindless effort to attach themselves to teacher and classmates all at once, like shipwrecked sailors grabbing for a life preserver. They look as if they want to lose themselves completely and become sheep.

Others are more selective and leisurely. They're also more efficient. They take the time and trouble to size up the environment and the personnel. Then they find their targets and lay out what they hope will be a winning campaign.

Some pave the way for the rest. They are the leaders. They are the models the rest emulate. They are the ones whose favors are courted.

Some don't care. They are born so independent, self-contained, inner-directed, or what have you, that the mainstream never has to be their stream.

Some become disoriented and disorganized and follow no rational, logical path. Sometimes they try very hard to get along. Sometimes, in temporary despair, or rage at failure, they try very hard to bust up the whole system.

Some are quietly and uncomplainingly overwhelmed and miserable. You will be horrified, perhaps, at what happens. You may be shocked to watch what seemed to be a sensible, sturdy little girl turn into a helpless blob, who can't think or even speak without prior approval from teacher or class leader. If your daughter is the leader, you may strongly disapprove of the way she loves her power and wields it, sometimes cruelly. If your child is overwhelmed and despairing, you'll begin to wonder how she will ever become a student.

In short, you'll get anxious. You will immediately want to "do" something. But remember, she's six. Remember what sixes are up to and what they have to learn. If you don't, you may misjudge the teacher, the classmates, and even your own child. Instead of helping her, you may get her off on the wrong track.

Conformity is the name of the game. Some children learn it faster than others. Some people never learn it at all. It may look silly to you, but it's important if you are six. You won't help your daughter by blaming her troubles on the system. Where does that leave a six-year-old except out of it? No matter how much you love and protect, your love and protection are no longer enough. They can't take the place of a secure status with teacher and classmates.

You can explain, nicely, to your daughter's teacher that you know your child and child development better than she does, and explain that she should prevent competition and let each child learn at his or her individual speed. But will that encourage the teacher to be more attentive to your child's need? More likely it will persuade her that she needs toughening up.

You can chastise your daughter for sacrificing her six-year-old principles to be popular. You may (1) say, "Fancy dresses like Diane's [the class leader's] are bad taste." You may (2) chide her for making fun of her old friends in the interest of gaining the star's approval. You may (3) shame her for bragging about how much better, faster, bigger her family's house, car, clothes, and so on, are. But you will do no more than make her feel guilty about what she has to do right now in spite of you.

You may think you've lost her and that all your loving efforts were in vain. Wait and see. Once she's found her way to belong she'll relax and come back to being herself. Keep out of the act as much as you can. Give her time to find her way before you worry about her progress—on all fronts.

Certain aspects of first grade life are a common focus of parent anxiety.

Competition

It seems ridiculous to encourage competition at this age, when children are trying so hard to fit in and learn how to learn. But children create competitive situations whether you encourage them or not. Many of them depend on marks the way they depend on leaders—for guides. These children stimulate the rest to compete. If you skipped the marks, children would find some other way of figuring out how teachers value their work. They're true detectives. "I got a smile in English," a granddaughter reported recently. "Johnny got nothing."

We're not advocating that first grade teachers set up competitive learning situations that make it uncomfortable or unnecessarily difficult for any child in the class to function easily. Nevertheless, the role that success and achievement play in our culture makes it seem unrealistic to expect our schools to be free of competition. If we accept the importance of recognizing individuality in children, we must accept differences in learning style and ability. Eliminating competition won't make the slow fast or the able less successful.

The ideal teacher will try to make sure that competition is fair and not foul, and she will make sure that it doesn't dominate school life. She will see to it that there is time in the school day for every single child to experience some moment of valid achievement and success.

Some children are naturally more competitive than others. This is not necessarily because they have been brought up in competitive families. They are ambitious and usually able, and compete against even their own past achievements. If there are no contests they manufacture them. They thrive on competition.

Others are completely indifferent. They don't need the stimulus of competition to learn. Their own interest and involvement pull them along and make them try to master and excel. When they're not interested, they won't work hard. They don't have to compete. They don't have to conform. They are the kind of children who go through first grade apparently immune to the power struggles going on around them.

Another group suffers from competition. It may almost paralyze them to match themselves to someone else's pace. Pushy parents are sometimes but by no means inevitably responsible. It's largely a matter of temperament. The child who is slow and tentative about exploring and assessing new tasks and making new friends needs time and space to get started. If you are anxious about achievement and constantly weigh her progress against the group's, you will make her anxious, too. Pressure of class competition has the same effect.

If your child is upset by competition, help her cope with it. Wishing it away won't work. Telling her that results don't matter is telling her a palpable untruth. They do matter—falsely or not—in determining one's status. If she stops trying to compete she'll stop trying for a place. She'll rely, instead, on her place with you. She won't progress. Besides, competition becomes more important as she goes along. It's easier to learn to handle it in first grade, where everything is relatively gentle and easy, than to put it off until failure makes a real difference.

At the bottom of most fear of competition is fear of being "outside." Teach your child how to handle competition systematically and coolly, just as you would teach any game. Make sure by word and deed that your daughter knows that her value and importance to you don't go up and down with her marks or her place in the class. Make sure she *wants* to compete and knows what she's working for. Then start very simply. For example, review the words and sounds she needs to know until she has mastered them securely. Try them over and over, casually, at well-spaced intervals, in short periods to match her attention span—while she's getting her room picked up or you're putting clothes away. When she is convinced she knows them, remind her that she'll know them just as well in class as she does at home. She may not get them perfect. But eventually progress will build confidence, and achievement will continue. She may never be able to recite as well as the natural competitor or the first scholar in her class. But, more important, she will have learned to use her abilities without being handicapped by fear.

Perhaps she has athletic or dramatic ambitions. She wants to be a prize swimmer or get the lead in the Thanksgiving pageant. One failure, however, and she gives up, too discouraged to face competition again. If you think she really cares about what she was trying for, you can help her persevere, in the same way you would help a first grader learn to prepare her lessons more effectively: (1) by showing her that doing well, mastering any skill, takes time and practice; (2) by helping her realize, through your encouragement and support, that you can have fun and success, too, without being the all-time winner or the star of every act.

Children are no different from the rest of humankind. Most of us have limited goals and ambitions. We don't all need to be first in our work or in the hearts of our countrymen. Once we make some friends and find our niche, we're pretty satisfied moving along somewhere beneath the top and comfortably clear of the bottom.

Private and Public

As we've discussed, the six-year-old's reliance on rules and models springs from the beginner's normal anxiety about making fatal missteps. At this age many children are not experienced and sophisticated enough to recognize subtle distinctions between what's acceptable in the privacy of the family and what's appropriate for public consumption. You can spare your daughter a good deal of gentle teasing and even grave embarrassment by coaching her.

You might want to talk now and then about *family*. If you give her examples from her own experience, she will quickly understand *how* your relationship with her and to each other is different and special. When she feels lonely, or falls down and hurts herself, she wants you. Her best friend's father and mother—no matter how close she feels to them—aren't the same. That's family. Because you are so close and important to each other, things you say and do are private—secrets—reserved for family only. You have your special family ways of doing things, taking care of each other and of her, and getting along. All families have their special ways, just as you do. They suit the family, but they are private—for family discussion, only.

You may have to be quite specific about what you don't want your child to talk about outside the family, particularly if she is on the younger side of this age range, and still socially inexperienced. So, in the course of your dinner table conversation or whatever conversation you plan to have about family privacy, say, "Don't tell Sara that Daddy got the great big raise we're celebrating, dear. We don't tell things like that to people we don't know very well."

When you're shaving in the morning and having your

usual catch-up conversation with your daughter who is having her morning B.M., remind her that some parents don't like to have their children in the bathroom with them. Tell her not to ask them why they don't. That's *their* private business.

If she says, "Sara's mother never lets her father in the kitchen," tell her, "That's their family style. It's best not to tell them we believe in sharing the work."

If both of you feel strongly about your equal roles in family life, make sure your daughter doesn't think she has to convert her friends' mothers and fathers to your ways.

Sex education: No two sets of parents are going to teach their children about their bodies and about sexual development, function, and behavior in the same way, or at the same time. People still have very strong feelings and fears on this subject. You may worry about making your daughter self-conscious by suggesting that sex education and discussion should be private. Quite the contrary. What might really shock and upset her would be a nonreceptive family's reaction if, not forewarned, she decided to share her latest gleanings on sex and body parts with them.

If you have made these kinds of distinction about "public" and "private" with your child, she'll take your advice without much questioning. She may tell her best friend a few things—explaining it's private—but the friend, if she's a real friend, will know what she can pass on to her parents.

Sexual Hazards

You may have similar qualms about warning your child of sexual hazards in the community. But the risk of giving her a morbid picture of sex is minimal compared with the risk of leaving her uninformed and unprotected. Besides, we repeat, children are matter-of-fact. If they are used to having sex treated in a straightforward manner, what you tell them won't make them anxious. Some children are more adventurous than others, but both boys and girls should learn where to go, where not to go, how to behave on the street (particularly when they are alone), and what to do in case of an approach from a stranger.

1. Remind her that people are not all good and kind, and some few are sick and dangerous.

2. Explain that there is no reason for her to worry about being hurt. If she follows your advice, there is nothing to fear.

3. Be explicit about where she should and should not go on her way to school, regular outside appointments, friends' houses. Direct her to go by the safest, most well traveled routes. Emphasize the dangerous streets, stores, and other spots, if any, that she should always avoid.

4. Tell her never to accept an offer of a ride from a stranger. If the stranger coaxes her, or gets out of the car, tell her to go to the nearest store and tell the storekeeper what's happened, or run to the nearest house.

5. Advise her not to speak to strangers on the street. If a stranger asks directions, she should give them, but never take the inquirer where he wants to go. Tell her never to accept candy or anything else from a stranger, or go into a building or store with anyone she doesn't know, for any reason.

6. If she gets sick or hurts herself, and she's alone, tell her to go to the nearest policeman, storekeeper, bus driver, or neighbor.

7. If she is ever frightened by a stranger's behavior, she should try to remember what the person looks like and

where she saw him, and tell you right away. Explain that you want to keep people like this from frightening children.

Halloween seems to have stimulated a certain amount of sadistic behavior against children in recent years. To be on the safe side, be sure your child does her trick-or-treating with a responsible older child or an adult. Know the group she goes with and make sure that all members understand that they must stay together. Tell your daughter not to eat anything she collects until you see and approve. Explain why.

If all this advice makes it sound as if we were living in a combat zone, maybe some of us, both urban and rural dwellers, are. Anyway, prepare your daughter to avoid muggings, *if* they are common in your community. The child who seems least vulnerable is the one who acts as if she had a destination in mind and keeps going toward it. The one who dawdles along absent-mindedly, apparently unaware of what's going on around her as she stops to window-shop, is a likely target.

Tell her to keep to main routes where there are people on the streets; travel in groups of two or three, when possible; stick close to grown-up pedestrians, if alone; watch out for potential muggers (they are often groups of older boys hanging around, rather than on the move). Above all, warn her not to resist. If accosted, she should hand over whatever is demanded quickly and quietly, move on to the nearest port of safety, and report what happened.

Sex, Sexuality, and Sex Roles

Little girls' fears about sex don't come from learning about child molesters and how to protect themselves. Quite the contrary, we think.

There is no way to shelter girls from their particular vul-

81

nerability. Child molesters exist. They are almost always men, and their victims are almost always girls. These are the facts. In the opinion of social psychologists, this reality explains why parents protect and supervise their daughters more carefully than their sons.

Little girls inevitably become aware, very early in life, of the attraction and risk being female creates for them, in the same way that every woman knows that her body, as distinct from her person and her own sexuality, makes her a target for the rapist.

In the past, parents protected and supervised more rigorously than they do now, but the facts were concealed. The little girl knew her vulnerability, but she didn't understand it. In the context of all the restrictions and prohibitions that she experienced: against masturbating, letting her panties show, punching her boy playmate, staying out after dark, climbing trees, asking why the dog is stuck in his friend or why Mommy has blood in her pants, her felt but unexplained vulnerability came to seem an ineradicable flaw—a badge of shame over which she had no control. She felt guilty, helpless, and unworthy. These feelings were intensified by the role she was taught to play in life. They haunt many women forever—interfering with judgment, enjoyment, and fulfillment in sex and trust and satisfaction in close relationships, and inhibiting expressiveness, assertiveness, and achievement.

Your daughter is growing up under entirely different auspices. The sexual climate has changed. Today's parents don't slap baby hands when they reach for the delight of the clitoris. They don't scold little girls for trying to satisfy their perfectly natural curiosity about their bodies, your bodies, and the normal processes of life. They try to be attentive and responsive to their daughters' individuality as to their developing sexuality. The tree climbers climb. The scientists dissect frogs. The active play football with the boys. Girls assert themselves and express themselves as freely and uninhibitedly as their brothers.

As you know, a child's feelings about herself, her body, and her sexuality are all inextricably intertwined. They nourish each other and so we try to nourish them all.

So girls, today, see their vulnerability quite differently. It is no cause for shame. It doesn't limit them. It doesn't make them inferior. It is a fact to be taken into account, rather than an ominous "sentence." Learning about molesters teaches them how to protect themselves. It makes them feel competent and safe, rather than exposed and helpless.

In first grade, as children enter the age of conformity, parents worry about the influence of the outside world. You hear the language your children bring home. You see the TV they insist they have to watch so they can talk to their friends. You've carefully kept your children from becoming soft-drink addicts. Now the mass pressure is irresistible. You may also fear that your daughter's attitudes and feelings about herself that you have so carefully nurtured may be at stake.

Tim's mother calls up. She sounds as if your six-year-old were a scheming woman out to steal her son. She tells you about the sex play she found going on in her house. Obviously, Tim's mother has scolded and scared. What can you do to undo the damage? Just what you've always done. Keep cool and calm. Treat the incident casually. Although children are supposed to be uninterested in each other at this age, it is actually, as you may remember, a period of active exploration. It probably won't do your daughter or the boy she has allegedly seduced any more harm than it did you when you were her age. However, little boys' mothers tend to be very fearful for their sons' safety. Calm the mother by telling her that you have heard this kind of thing is fairly normal. Then assure her that you will talk to your daughter. Make sure that your daughter understands this is not to happen again.

Ask her what she and Timmy were doing that Mrs. T. didn't like. She'll tell you. "He was looking at my vagina [or wee wee, or whatever you call it in your family], and I was seeing his penis. I felt it. It doesn't look like Daddy's."

You will have to laugh. Then you can explain that Timmy is small, so his penis is small and it will grow when he grows. We can't put words in your mouth. But you see, not only can you keep the incident from becoming traumatic; you can use it to help answer her natural questions in a perfectly natural way. Then you can tell her, as you probably have about many other things, that this is something most parents don't like their children to do; vaginas and penises are private. If she has any more questions she'll ask them sooner or later. She may do more exploring, but she won't let Timmy examine her again. You can tell that to his mother. If you handle the incident in this way, your child won't be much more intimidated by Mrs. T.'s scolding than she would have been if Mrs. T. had punished Timmy and her for taking ice cream without asking.

In these impressionable years teachers' attitudes may be a more serious cause for concern. In subtle and not so subtle ways they often define for boys and girls their respective roles. And you may fear that in her zeal to be a proper first grader, to have a place, your daughter will sacrifice the free spirit you have so carefully cultivated.

In 1974 Eleanor Emmons Maccoby, Chairman of the Department of Psychology at Stanford University, and Carol Nagy Jacklin, a research associate in the department, published a comprehensive survey and analysis of more than 1,400 study papers on sex differences that had appeared over the previous ten years. The survey produced the astonishing information that, almost without exception, previously held convictions about differences in boys' and girls' early cognitive abilities were unsubstantiated in fact. Differences that did exist were found to be so insignificant as to be immaterial.[1]

Two commonly accepted differences were confirmed by the studies surveyed: girls have better memories for verbal content—particularly after age seven—and boys are better at remembering spatial designs.

The survey further revealed that divergences in cognitive abilities develop rapidly in adolescence, until at college age boys are well ahead of girls in a good many of the skills needed for advanced academic work, particularly in mathematics and the sciences.

There are no conclusive explanations for the deceleration in girls' cognitive growth. Some experts relate the change to hormonal factors. More persuasive, perhaps, are studies suggesting that girls' models (mothers) and cultural pressures that discourage girls from assertiveness and achievement make them fearful of success and thus exert a suppressive influence on ambition and effort.

The Women's Liberation movement has brought about amazing changes in ten brief years. As mothers continue to expand their horizons, girls will continue to change to fit the models. As fathers' attitudes change, so will their expectations of daughters. As women push society to eliminate the strictures that have curbed women's aspirations and efforts, girls' other goal-setters—their teachers—will change, too.

In this time of transition, however, the old models, the old stereotypes, still have a powerful hold.

When we were starting elementary school, the teachers' favorite girls helped clean up the classroom, while the boys went out to play baseball. We remember cleaning erasers—a top honor. We were appreciative, in spite of the lungs full of chalk dust, although we would have preferred to carry the flag in assembly (a boys' honor). However, we would gladly have dispensed with *all* honors for a chance to play baseball with the HEROES.

We didn't think this was unfair. We didn't even question why we couldn't do what we chose to, what we knew we could do as well as boys. We accepted it. That's what first graders do. We were outsiders, lesser than boys. We satisfied ourselves fighting for position in our cliques.

Recently, at a girls' school, we watched first graders weaving, shaping clay into bowls and pitchers and baskets, doing needlework, making furniture.

One child was working with extraordinary skill and speed on a dollhouse that the class was building. It was a remarkable piece of construction: the doors and windows precisely cut out of the walls with a jigsaw and then neatly hinged back on to open and shut; the stair well neatly planned and waiting for steps. Not many children were as accomplished as this particular carpenter. But there were obviously several in the group who wanted to try.

We thought of this later in a first grade in a middle-sized midwestern city where another dollhouse was going up. Here the boys had the tools and the girls were making curtains. We asked why none of the girls were hammering. The teacher laughed as if we were making a joke. "We never thought of *that*," she said. "We teach sewing."

Surely there were girls here who could build as well as the boys or would like a chance to try. But the girls were doing what they found was expected. If they see that they are not expected to try carpentry, they usually don't.

This is how role casting begins. Perhaps innocently— through habit, formed by their own experience and training —teachers repeat *their* teachers, just as daughters repeat their mothers. They probably often don't even really see or hear what they are doing and saying.

A girl can't very well get to know *her*self, when *a* self is prescribed for her in first grade or earlier. Six-year-olds should have a chance to *choose* what they try in free time.

There isn't any objective reason for teaching girls differently from boys. Nevertheless, in many first grade classrooms across the country, girls are getting the same old girls' lessons and boys are getting special boys' lessons, right with their phonics.

Little girls and little boys are both carefully taught that the so-called female talents for handwork and human relations make *them* models of dependability and conformity. Little girls are held up to little boys as examples of how to behave, how to do good work, how to make nice, neat papers and nice, clear writing.

It's hard to say how much classroom and community attitudes will influence your particular daughter. You have to make that evaluation yourself. Your counterinfluence, her personality, the strength of her abilities, interest and drive will all enter in.

However, if you feel that school and teacher attitudes are potentially discouraging to girls, and you feel it strongly, do something. Don't barge in and try to turn the teacher around. This would only embarrass your daughter and antagonize the teacher. The more effective approach would be to work with your friends in the PTA, if there is one, or, if not, through the superintendent's or principal's office or the Board of Education. As we've said, teachers often act heedlessly. A little consciousness raising is all they need to change their ways.

You can make your own list of suggestions for change, to fit the situation in your school. Here are a few to help you get started.

1. Choose boys as often as girls for helping jobs—cleaning up after snacks or art period, watering plants. Use boys as often as girls as examples of neatness, careful work, good behavior, reliability, gentleness.

2. Choose girls as often as boys in impromptu class dramatics to play roles traditionally filled by boys (doctors, lawyers, engineers, architects, scientists).

3. Call on girls to take responsibility for class matters beyond the food, decorating, and cleaning areas. For example, why not choose a boy to plan the menu now and then, a girl to compute the party costs or the amount of lumber needed for a hamster cage. Choose a girl to decide what the letter to Bob, who is in the hospital, should say, rather than simply to copy it; to head the committee to plan the spring camping trip instead of to plan and buy the food.

4. Call on boys as often as girls to pass cookies, introduce class guests, accompany a child who is upset or ill to the nurse, and so on.

5. Make sure library books promote contemporary views of men's and women's roles. If you don't feel your parent group is ready for this kind of assertiveness, you can make sure you keep your daughter's options open until she can decide how she wants to play her female role, by what you say and do at home. It means keeping an open house where everyone shares the responsibility, the fun, and the privileges, according to interest, ability, and choice, rather than being assigned jobs and privileges by sex. In such families, girls understand—from the time they first *do* understand—that childhood is a time to plan for life. They learn right along with their brothers that school, books, and all the experiences of music, art, crafts, theater, and athletics that their parents expose them to are ways to find out what they like, what they are good at. This kind of exposure stimulates them to think about how they might want to make a living and a life when they are grown up and independent.

Girls have neither weakness nor handicap to keep them from going where they please—only their individual constitutional limitations, and what their parents and teachers teach them. In the years from six to nine, when children are so busy learning their own best ways to accommodate to the demands of their society and their peers, the expectations you have for your daughter, the freedom you give her to explore, and the support you give her efforts will have a significant influence on her goals and her enthusiasm for the challenges she will face to achieve them.

Q. How much should we expect our first grader to learn? As far as we can tell, she is still learning to write her numbers and letters and identify a few consonant and vowel sounds, and the year is half over.

A. School systems vary in what they expect of first grade children.

Find out from the teacher what *she* expects and whether your daughter is making satisfactory progress. There is no hurry about learning to read in first grade, as long as the foundation for learning is being laid down. See *How to Help Your Child Get the Most Out of School* for a fuller answer.[2]

Q. We have heard that it is dangerous for fathers to take too much interest in their daughters at this age. Why?

A. We can't imagine. All we know is that daughters seem to get as much spirit and drive from their fathers' encouragement as from their mothers' ability to let them test their wings alone, wander and explore. Fathers and daughters obviously have a special relationship. We can't see how it would have any negative effects unless a father (a) tried to substitute a daughter for the son he wanted to have, or (b) used her as a partner to put down her mother.

It is always important to children that their parents agree, basically, on how to raise their children, and support each other in discipline and training. Of course, the system breaks down now and then. Don't worry about that. Try to settle your disagreements in private, however, when possible.

Q. Our daughter takes quarters from my change purse or her father's pocket. When we ask her why she does it she tells us that she lost her allowance. We don't believe her explanation and we are concerned that dishonesty will become a habit.

A. Tell her to let you know when she loses her allowance and you will replace it. Warn her, however, that you expect her to learn to take care of it. As you suspect, this is not the real reason that she takes money. It's fairly typical for children to try to buy friendship at this age, when they are still new to the social scene. In the same way they sometimes lie to you about their marks, their friendships, and their progress. You might talk to your daughter's teacher about how she is getting along and see whether the teacher has any practical suggestions that might help your daughter feel less pressure to make her mark in her work and with her friends. Don't be harsh and punitive. The problem is not serious at this stage. If she continues to take money you should let her know that you don't really accept her excuses and want her to stop. Usually this behavior is short-lived.

NOTES

[1] Eleanor Emmons Maccoby and Carol Nagy Jacklin, *The Psychology of Sex Differences* (Stanford, Calif.: Stanford University Press, 1974).

The survey and analysis of 1,400 research papers on sex differences published since 1965 challenges the following widely held beliefs:

1. Girls are supposed to learn more easily than boys do by hearing and seeing.

"The case for a greater 'hunger for auditory stimulation among girls has not been proved'" (p. 27).

"From the first birthday to adulthood, the very large majority of studies report no sex difference in visual perception" (p. 28).

"The two sexes are very similar in their interest in and utilization of information that comes to them via hearing and vision" (p. 35).

2. Girls are thought to have more verbal aptitude. They are said to read earlier, while boys are thought to be more skilled at math.

"Sex differences in reading and arithmetic achievement are minimal during the early school years" (p. 35).

3. Girls are supposed to be more responsive to social stimulus than boys—an explanation often offered for their talent for people and their imitative, co-operative, rather than independent, assertive, behavior.

Maccoby and Jacklin find no support. Nor could they find that boys are more responsive to *things*.

They confirmed only two commonly accepted differences. They found that girls have better memories for verbal content —particularly after age seven—and that boys are better at remembering spatial designs. But they finally conclude that "it cannot clearly be said that either sex has a superior memory capacity, or set of skills in the storage and retrieval of information when a variety of content is considered" (p. 59).

[2] Stella Chess, M.D., and Jane Whitbread, *How to Help Your Child Get the Most Out of School* (Garden City, N.Y.: Doubleday & Company, 1974; New York: Dell, 1976).

CHAPTER SIX

Betwixt and Between

Nine to Twelve

Nine is the peak of childhood. Twelve is almost grown-up. At this stage, girls can look, feel, and act five, twenty-five, or any other age along the way.

Ask an eleven-year-old what she thinks her best year was and she'll say, unhesitatingly, "Now." Then, if she can stand off a little and see the humor in herself, she may smile a little and add, "I would have said that last year and the year before last, too."

Some girls hate being this age, of course, but they're few and far between. It's a very good age for girls and it's an even better age for parents to watch and enjoy.

Profile

At nine, girls are usually taller than boys. But this is only the most noticeable evidence that they're temporarily ahead of boys in development. They are also more sophisticated.

They have more grace, poise, self-awareness, perception, and understanding. Their social skills are more advanced than boys', as a rule.

Nines are in fourth grade—a turning point in school. In fourth grade open-corridor teaching, ungraded classes, and comment-style report cards usually stop. This is the year that teachers start giving serious homework and students learn to make time charts of events and developments around the world at the period they're studying, to help them put the history of the country they're learning about in the proper perspective. It's the time when they begin to study science and plan experiments to demonstrate the basic scientific laws. It's the grade when, having supposedly mastered the fundamental tools of knowledge, they begin to gobble up information at a fantastic rate.

Boys aren't always ready to buckle down to the new demands of fourth grade. They're not always well prepared, or focused, or able to concentrate. Creeping like snails, as in Shakespeare's day, they advance somewhat unwillingly toward maturity—in school and out. Spitballs, slingshots with paper clips, the bean shooter and water pistol, the foot in the aisle to trip the eager beaver's progress to the blackboard, typify boys' classroom behavior, more often than girls'.

Girls behave as if they'd been lying in wait for the opportunities that fourth grade presents to be older, more advanced, more mature. Even if they're not the prize students, they are usually conscientious and diligent ones. The content of their papers may lack something in understanding or execution, but the papers *look* beautiful. Depending, of course, on individual temperament, girls can be almost obsessive. In their anxiety about making their work look perfect they will copy, recopy, and copy again, sometimes losing sight of the question they're supposed to be dealing with in the process. Good students are capable of incredible concentration and maturity of thought and organization. When one twelve-year-old we know was asked to remember her fourth grade self her eyes sparkled with delight. "It felt so good being able to find out and think and work as hard as I could. Before that, someone was always interrupting you or showing you her work. You always heard everyone's conversations and you *had* to stop and listen. Finally in fourth grade I had a quiet classroom and I could do things by myself and I could work as hard as I wanted to."

Girls' eagerness to grow up and try the tasks of maturity is not limited to school performances. At this age they are looking for all kinds of challenges. They are eager for riding lessons, tennis, piano, clarinet, ballet. If they like reading, they become insatiable readers. This may be because they read earlier and more easily than boys do, in general, but it's also because they're already wondering what kinds of lives they'll choose, how they're going to fit into the adult world.

At nine very few children of either sex have any strong convictions about what they'll do when they grow up, but girls, more often than boys, are entertaining possibilities. In their earlier years they model themselves blindly after their teachers and their mothers. One girl says, "When I was in first grade I was going to be a first grade teacher when I grew up, and in second grade a second grade teacher. Now I get my ideas from books. If I read about a reporter, I think I'll be a journalist. If I read about a nurse, I consider medicine. I think I'm really trying out different careers for fit. I know I don't want to stay home all day. I want to be something."

In the classroom, girls and boys usually get traditional jobs, still. The boy will usually be president, the girl secretary, but the girl will probably be more efficient about organizing and administering the class business—assigning jobs and seeing that they get done, keeping records and balancing books.

The relative maturity of girls at this age is most apparent in their social behavior. Boys can handle themselves as long as they're in action. Tennis players can talk endlessly about tennis with tennis friends. A boy will become wholly absorbed in whatever sport he's interested in, planning strategy, practicing, and analyzing tactics and plays with his teammates.

On an overnight camp-out with girls, boys are splendidly co-operative and efficient about doing "men's work"—laying out the campsite, building fires, burying garbage, and stowing gear fast in a race against an impending cloudburst.

Then, once the dinner's over and cleaned up and the campfire is roaring, they're at a loss. One or two of the more mature twelve-year-olds may be able to join the girls gracefully, talk, play games, sing, participate in serious or funny discussions. The rest will spend the evening throwing cornhusks at each other, knocking each other down or into a group of girls, wrestling, name calling.

The girls treat them with the amused tolerance of the superior and powerful. They beg the boys to stop being "babies" or "clowns." Then they turn back to their own business.

But, if they are physically, mentally, and emotionally older than the boys, girls are by no means all grown up. At any time during this age span it's not at all unusual for a girl to declare a sudden moratorium on growing up. Woe to the parent who has disposed of the trappings of a daughter's *apparently* cast-off childhood when this happens. Out of the blue a nine-, ten-, or twelve-year-old will rescue her doll family from the back of the closet where it has been languishing and begin a total replay of her earlier years. She bathes her dolls, grooms their hair, washes and irons their wardrobes, scrubs, perhaps even repaints her doll furniture and redecorates her dollhouse if she had one.

She may revive, overnight, her best friendship with the boy next door whom she hasn't so much as nodded to of late. The two may spend an uninterrupted weekend playing catch, or working in a forgotten sandbox with the blocks and rusty trucks of yore. Then, almost wistfully—or so it seems to the parents who may hate to see childhood end for their daughter, too—she'll come home from school one day, throw all the baby stuff back in the discard heap, and resume her march toward maturity.

These acts of play, like all play, are in a sense symbolic. They dramatize the pulls and tugs that girls experience during these in-between years. The fact that they are closer to physical maturity than boys are at the same age may make them more conscious than their brothers of the passage of time, more anxious about what the future will bring to them, less able to cling to childhood, and still a bit unwilling to leave it. Boys, of course, have similar feelings as they approach adolescence, but in our culture they have already learned to conceal emotions. And perhaps this helps them ignore, or at least suppress, their ambivalent feelings about growing up.

It's hard for girls to ignore the imminence of menstruation and the visible signs of impending maturity they see in themselves—sometimes as early as nine or ten, and almost inevitably by thirteen. The questions that budding breasts, the appearance of pubic and underarm hair, and the new feelings toward boys stimulate may be too vague to put into words or even to be fully aware of, but they cause discomfort and insecurity, now and then.

The most independent eight-year-old, for example, can become, at ten, a slave to popular trends in language, dress, interests, and associations. The devoted pianist will abandon practice, refuse lessons, demand a clarinet. The ballet student who was going to be a ballerina will drop ballet and switch to tap. She will beg for a skirt with fringe one week, then refuse to wear it the next, insisting on pants with legs of an exact width and cut, and none other. A new word—"gross," for example—will slip into her vocabulary and instantly provide an all-purpose complete vocabulary. Whether applied to the weather, the family's weekend plans, the new teacher, or the dress you've just purchased, its meaning is the same: unacceptable.

Socially, boys may exhibit the generalized physical lack of togetherness that girls describe as "babyish," "clownish," or "gross." Their pants always seem to be falling. They are always losing sweaters and jackets, and especially their schoolbooks. But, while girls appear to have much more social know-how, they are characteristically cliquy, disloyal, cruel, insecure, and a bit bitchy now. Today's best friend becomes tomorrow's discard. Parents watch in horror at what seem to be total personality changes in previously lovely, upright little girls. Sometimes girls are just as unsettled by their behavior as the disapproving elders who watch them. Sometimes they are unregenerate, relishing their freewheeling and dealing.

Sarah, Alice, Laura, and Joan were a solid foursome of eleven-year-olds we saw in a school we visit from time to time. They helped each other with homework. They promoted one another for class offices. They played together in gym periods, where they were among the better class athletes. If one girl bought a striped shirt, they all bought striped shirts. They spent every afternoon not pre-empted by piano, recorder, violin, clarinet, gymnastic, or tennis lessons, or dental or doctor appointments, at each other's houses, eating, talking, playing cards, and studying, in unalterable order. They spent one hour, religiously, after dinner on the phone with one other, deciding what to wear the next day, or how to do the homework, or why it was unfair.

During spring vacation Sarah went to Bermuda with her parents. The day after school resumed, her best friends cut her dead. When she sat down for lunch with them they stopped talking. When she joined them after school they explained with too much politeness that they had started a science project that was too far along for her to get into. No one ever called her after dinner.

She sorrowed alone for a week, unable to tell her parents what had happened. The next week she recovered sufficiently to dredge up a last-year's friend whom she had abandoned when she made the "in" group.

Two days later, Alice's interest in Sarah revived. She asked her over after school. Sarah brought her NEW old friend. The next day she told the NEW old friend she would be busy on "something" for a while and redropped her. The following day the former foursome regrouped. The whole class was absorbed in the pre-teen soap opera unfolding around them.

At this point a reporter writing on the pre-teen scene visited and asked to talk to some sixth graders. The teacher produced the feuding foursome because they were among the most articulate girls in the class.

"As I remember," the reporter began, "at your age girls are always worrying about who their friends are and fighting a lot for status. True? False."

"True," they answered as one, laughing. "We're fighting right now." Then all of them tried to describe what was going on. As they saw it, one or the other of them did something every day that was provocative or upsetting to someone. Joan imagined Alice had snubbed Laura. Sarah ac-

99

cused Laura of pretending not to hear when she said hi. Laura said that when she said hi Sarah did not say hi back. Alice said Sarah used a funny tone when she called to ask about homework. Joan said Alice brought chocolate chip cookies for lunch when she knew Alice couldn't eat them. No one was aware of doing what she was accused of.

They all knew that the reasons they were giving for feuding were nonsense. They couldn't find any real explanation for the fighting, but they couldn't stop. The interview gave them a chance to face themselves together. They saw their foolishness. The next day they reformed and became as solid as before. However, if you know much about eleven-year-olds or nine-, ten-, or, to a lesser extent, twelve-year-olds, you would not vouch for the permanence of the alliance.

You just can't predict the course of friendship among girls at this age. There's a need—varying in intensity according to the individual—for Gibraltar-like attachments in this betwixt-and-between period. Impressive sophistication and maturity exist side by side with fearsome anxiety about the changing body, the person-to-be. The "best friends" are anchors against these tides of confusion. When anything real or imagined threatens the anchorage, a girl can be almost as upset as a two-year-old who can't find her baby blanket at bedtime.

This dependence on attachments explains a variety of inconsistent behavior, dogged devotion to unworthy companions or to leaders, preoccupation with one's social, athletic, and academic rank and the status of one's group.

Girls will latch on to friends their parents can't believe they enjoy and drop the friends they really love because they're too young, too small, not developed enough, not popular enough, from the wrong part of town, or not equipped with the right kind of jeans, shoes, hairstyles, or family car. They'll go into a decline, or pretend to, because they imagine the friend that's closest or the leader of the group they *thought* they were in did not say the right thing or give the right look. They exhibit taste, behavior, and standards you can't believe of them on Monday, then become self-righteous on Tuesday and condemn someone else for the identical behavior. You can almost always trace the sudden shift in gears to the need to curry favor with a new rising star in the class.

They need the support and backing of a group to relieve their anxieties about who they are and who they're going to be. Nevertheless, you can't describe the average pre-teen girl as a tragic heroine. A lot of the melodrama she exudes is pure fun and games. She played out childhood relationships and problems with doll families. Now she experiments with relationships, ways of behaving, attitudes, tastes, and styles with her peers. An actress reading a part for the first time tries many ways to say the same line before she settles into the one she believes suits the character and situation best. There's an aspect of the rehearsing actress about the girl on the verge of her teens. Playfully, she is starting to try out ways to be a grown-up person.

Needs

Babies are fun just because they are new and also because they change so much and so fast that being with them is a constant string of surprises. But life with a daughter of nine through twelve is a special experience for parents, particularly mothers. In a daughter's looks, actions, attitudes, passions, loves, and hates, in her fears and her foibles, a mother will see herself at the same age. You are far enough away to have some perspective on what your daughter is going through. Still, you are close enough, if reminded, to feel it all again. You can remember the fun, excitement, pain, nastiness, vulgarity, and overblown emotion you experienced when you were her age, taking a look at the adult world and trying out for a place in it. You can love all the best in your daughter and view the worst with amused patience, knowing that it is purely temporary.

Most girls at this stage of development need very little more from you. If they had a reasonably good start in life they are amazingly well endowed at nine or ten to find their way along by themselves. Nevertheless, they need support and guidance. They value and depend on your awareness of their needs and your willingness to pay attention and listen. The temptation of parents, however, is to go further: to interfere too soon and too much. This makes children feel they aren't getting a chance to become independent. The trick, which requires the combined skills of a tightrope walker and a cordon bleu chef frying a plain egg, is to take your daughter seriously, without taking everything she says and does every minute seriously.

Two-year-olds, if you remember, are constantly testing. Parents in their darker moments see this as a challenge to their own sanity, endurance, and fitness to be parents. If they're not careful they forget to look at behavior from the child's view. Two-year-olds don't mean everything they say. They are just trying things out to find the right way for them. While they are getting to know the ropes and themselves they experiment with actions as they do with new words, to learn their capabilities and find their ways to get along. Children go through a similar experience in puberty as they face the adult world. They are getting to know the ropes, testing their own abilities, character, and nature. They don't mean everything they do and say. They are trying things on for fit. '

When a child is two you try to exert the patience, sensitivity, and skill that will keep you from swooping down every minute to yank, scream, hit, lecture, restrain. The two-year-old is climbing toward the open window ledge, reaching for the forbidden piece of candy, pulling the cat's tail; she is out of the yard and heading into the street and an oncoming car. She's about to spill her milk for the third time, watching you out of the corner of her eye.

When can you look the other way? When do you bear down? Experience, instinct, and/or exhaustion teach you to overlook a lot and stand firm on a few essentials. Your well-tempered guiding efforts keep your adventurous, enthusiastic, active, ever-learning toddler from becoming passive, docile, and limp, without drive, will to learn, or interest in your company. Your skillful handling keeps her from turning into a bundle of rebellion and unfocused negativism, getting her kicks out of grownups' anger rather than their pleasure and approval. And with experience and growing understanding she gradually learns how to operate relatively easily and peacefully in her world.

There is a parallel between the twos and the tens. Tens are trying to test their abilities again, sizing up and experimenting to discover how to fit in. They don't mean everything they do and say. They are just testing.

Too much negative pressure from parents interrupts and interferes with the process. It's like too much verbal instruction and physical direction when you're learning a sport. In order to make new lessons a confident part of you, you have to do a lot of the practicing on your own.

Take a good deal of your daughter's behavior with a grain of salt. Try to handle the really outrageous as matter-of-factly as you would a mistake in grammar or spelling. Stopping to remember what's behind the zigs and zags in behavior, values, and taste is half the battle, perhaps. If you realize that she won't always want to wear overstuffed bras and four-inch platform soles, or tie up the phone for hours to discuss today's chapter in the ongoing battle with teacher, you won't find it all so hard to ignore. You'll have the perspective you need to judge when and how to contribute positively.

Problem Solving

Maybe she's snubbing her best friend and wearing lipstick in school, besides. To make it worse, the best friend is your best friend's daughter. Your best friend is full of vicarious pain for her eleven-year-old, Judy. She can't help asking you, "What's happened to Jill? Judy says she spends all her time with the tough crowd. I suppose that's why she didn't make the honor roll this term."

You answer, "It's the age, Marj"—trying to be cool. But can you keep your cool with Jill? Marj has made you anxious. You find yourself asking your daughter why she didn't make the honor roll. "It's a drag, Mom," she says breezily.

A few days later, against your judgment you ask her why she never calls Judy back. "She's a drag, Mom. She acts like a toddler." Breezy again.

Now you are really anxious. Could the daughter who only last week wanted to know how she could get to be an archaeologist become a non-student to be popular?

Could the child whose loyalty to friends and siblings was sterling be dropping her best friend to get in with the most grown-up (measured by training bras size) crowd?

Well, she could, but it's only temporary, ninety-nine times out of one hundred. The best insurance that it *will* be transient is by treating it as if it were, by taking it lightly.

We saw this happen with a girl a few years ago. She dropped her best friend when a group of slightly older girls courted her. They needed a pitcher for their softball team and Suzy, coached by her father, was a star. The team became her life.

Her old friend kept calling. Suzy never called *her*. Her mother couldn't endure this betrayal of friendship. "Why don't you play with Judy any more?" she asked one day.

"She smells," Suzy answered, happily, using her all-purpose expression of the month.

"When did she start smelling?" her mother answered coolly.

That brought a smile. "The other kids don't like her," Suzy explained.

Still cool, her mother asked, "Do you?"

Now Suzy was embarrassed. She had to face her breach of loyalty. "I want to play softball," she said, sounding a little belligerent.

A few days later her mother suggested asking Judy to go swimming with them on Saturday. Suzy's answer was, "*Yuk.*"

Realizing she was not getting anywhere, her mother sensibly dropped the issue.

Suzy and her mother usually get dinner together while the younger children take their baths. This interval after she gets home from work is the time mother has reserved to keep in touch with daughter. Inevitably the girls on the team finally came into the conversation and Suzy's mother found out that their clothes, talents, possessions, and abilities were all superior. They sounded larger than life. With a lot of listening and a minimal amount of prying, she began to discern the cracks in the woodwork. Suzy was beginning to be worried about some of their ideas and the fact that they didn't like anything she liked except softball.

At this point her mother had sense enough to keep still. Instead of saying, "I told you so," or, "Why don't you drop

them?" she said, "It takes time to choose real friends."
Nothing more.

When the spring season began, Suzy wanted to get out of
the game. She stayed in because her teammates accused her
of deserting them when it was too late to get a substitute.

Suddenly Suzy began to be anxious about her schoolwork, where only a few months earlier she had been anxious that doing it would interfere with her standing on the
team. Then summer took care of everything.

The family came back from vacation the day before
school opened. Suzy's old best friend picked her up in the
morning as if there'd never been an interlude. Suzy hugged
her fondly. The softball crowd faded away. That year Suzy
and her friend were in the theater crowd. Suzy sent for catalogues from all the drama schools in the country.

Now she's twelve. She and the same old friend are going
to be photographers. Suzy's number two in her class—up
from next to the bottom. The other day her mother heard
her telling her nine-year-old sister to stay out of cliques and
choose her friends on her own. Suzy learned that on *her*
own (almost), and the knowledge is probably there to stay.
Developing your own standards, instead of doing what
you're told, is the way to independence and maturity.

When to Be Firm

Of course, girls at this still-tender age can't always be allowed to learn by themselves. If they're doing something
that threatens health, safety, and future, shuts off options,
or interferes with other people's rights and comfort, you
have to tug on the reins.

While no parent wants to or should ride herd on children
every moment they're in sight, every family has its own

rules, reflecting the parents' style and values, and these rules must be *fairly* consistently and evenhandedly enforced.

If you all share the chores, for example, you can't let the lazy one, or the clever one, or the fantastically busy and social one skip her duties.

You may outlaw scapegoating, bullying, provocation, tattling, certain types of discourtesy and rudeness, cruelty of all kinds. These standards have to be enforced most of the time to become established.

Children who have been brought up to assume increasing responsibility for themselves as they mature don't need lectures and lengthy explanations for family rules. They generally accept them easily. More often, it's the child who has so many rules that she can't think for herself who wants to forget or fight them all.

You probably won't let your daughter pick her time to come home at night or go to bed. You will probably want to know where she is, whom she's with, and when to expect her home after school, a party, or a date with a friend.

At this age, girls have neither the experience, nor the sophistication, nor the judgment—particularly at the lower end of the age range—to travel alone anywhere at any time. They are physically and emotionally vulnerable to deviant members of the community.

You should probably declare certain conduct, company, and places off bounds.

Because girls this age are still inexperienced, tentative about values, and easily influenced by their peers, they need clear guidance and explicit prohibitions about alcohol, tobacco, marijuana, and pills and drugs. The dangers of each and every class of stimulant, drug, and hallucinogen should be carefully spelled out. It is important to explain the physical risks involved in experimenting and the legal risks of buying or selling these substances or having them in their possession.

Moralizing and scare tactics are unnecessary; the facts are impressive in themselves. You never know what you are buying when you buy an illegal substance. You never know what you are getting when you take what is illegal. We know of one child this age who bought what she thought were pep pills. In reality they were sleeping pills. The dangers of taking unknown drugs are obvious. The dangers of addiction are obvious; although all takers always say they can control what they take, addiction is a fact of contemporary life. The dangers of experimenting with any unknown substance, of using any substance that has unpredictable effects on mind and body, without strict medical supervision are obvious. Children who play with alcohol and drugs risk their health and their lives. They risk their futures. Owning, buying, and selling are against the law. The penalties can be severe. You should be able to list them precisely and make clear the possible results of conviction on your daughter's development and her chance to pick the life she wants to lead.

Even if you have warned your daughter when she was younger about talking to strangers or going anywhere with a stranger under any condition, tell her again. Now you can be more explicit about the dangers involved. Preface your warning as we suggested you do earlier, with the statement that most people are normal and decent. Then remind her of the simple precautions to take in order to avoid problems with the rare man or woman who might frighten or harm her:

1. *Do not* talk to strangers on the street.

2. *Do not* open the door to anyone whose voice you don't recognize.

3. If a stranger asks direction or help, *do not* go with that person, off the street, to show the way.

4. *Do not* accept rides or gifts or offers from anyone whom you don't know.

5. *Do not* go with anyone you don't know anywhere for any reason.

6. *When in trouble* or need of help, call home or go to someone you know—a storekeeper, bank teller, librarian, or policeman.

7. *If you think you are being followed* or see a suspicious person on the street, go to a storekeeper, policeman, or other adult you know for help.

We have outlined the minimal guidelines most parents will want to use to help a daughter learn how to protect herself and become a responsible human being.

Discipline Without Don'ts

If the discussion seems short on rules and methods of enforcement, this is intentional. We don't think children follow rules and avoid punishment as much as they follow people and try to emulate them. Most human beings take criticism and advice more easily from someone they like and trust. When a bully and a cheat tells you to be kind and honest it isn't very convincing.

Children are people. What your daughter thinks of you or feels about you will influence her more than the rules you give her. If she's learned to love and trust you in her early years, she'll probably listen to you now and imitate your behavior and adopt your values.

Of course you'll have competition. At periods in development when children are between what they were and what they're going to be they are particularly vulnerable. Peer pressures press harder. What they *want* to do and be is not always what they are able to achieve. If you lay down the law, issue commands, and lecture instead of listening to your daughter, you don't really help. You cut off the advice she might ask for and the support she might get if you first heard her side and listened to her questions. If she has learned that confiding in you is safe and talking to you helpful, she'll continue to talk when she is in doubt or conflict. Then you may have the chance to help her find a semi-independent way to adolescence.

At this age, in contrast to adolescence, girls still want to know their parents and hear what they think. You are the influential ones if you want to be. Girls, now, want to hear your point of view and find out how you got to be what you are and what you are doing. They like their fathers and mothers to be interested in what *they're* doing and planning. They like to know what you think of their thoughts.

Many parents, however, are so busy making a living and providing the advantages they think all children need that they may forget to look and listen until they have to. Fathers, particularly, tend to stick to business unless the principal is calling, marks drop below sea level, or behavior is outrageous and Mother has given up.

The Father They Wish They Had

Girls miss their fathers. Difficulty in getting close to fathers was one of the few problems the children we talked to mentioned repeatedly. It's one that we often hear about from the children we study and work with.

One child reported, "I know my father loves me, but I wish I could talk to him. He's always joking. If I show him my report card and I have two B's and three A's he'll say,

110

'Why not five A's?' If I get five A's he says, 'No A-pluses?' I know he's being funny. It's his way of saying he's satisfied, but I wish he were serious once in a while. I wish he'd talk to me. He could tell me how to do better in history. B is okay, but I could do better and I want to."

They put it in different ways. "My father is an architect," one girl said. "He works Saturdays. He brings his work home. I know it's because there are six of us and he never says no to school, camp, music, ballet—anything. But I wish I *knew* him better. I'd like to hear more about his work. I might want to design houses or maybe get into planning. It's very hard for me to talk to him. He's so busy, or he treats me like a child—as if why would I want to worry about anything as hard as what he does."

Another girl came home from camp with gold medals in swimming and diving. She was the singles champion for her age group in tennis. She even had a blue ribbon in riding for the first time.

"My father hardly noticed. When I showed him my prizes he smiled and said, 'That's nice' as if I was showing him my new party dress or something. Then he turned on TV. That was the end."

Why is a girl's relationship with her father so important? Why does she value it so highly?

The man of the house is the Man of the House, or has been until recently. Girls see that pleasing Daddy is important to their mothers. Like mother, like daughter: it becomes important to them.

But, as times are changing, more and more little girls are growing up with mothers who have lifetime careers (about half the mothers in America with children under eighteen have jobs). Even women who are houseworkers and full-time mothers are bringing up their daughters with the idea that they should be prepared for work before, during, or instead of marriage and motherhood—as *they* choose.

The years between nine and twelve are the years when girls start planning their grown-up lives. In sixth grade and junior high they begin to weigh career possibilities realistically against their developing tastes, talents, and interests.

Fathers are still considered the most important "doers" in our culture, and in most families they *are* that. Girls see them as the family authorities on careers, and so fathers' encouragement and counsel is important to them. When fathers don't take their daughters' achievements and plans seriously, girls sometimes have trouble taking themselves seriously.

On the edge of adolescence, girls begin to feel a new kind of attraction to boys. They wonder what boys will think of them. They start to wonder about themselves in love, in marriage, as mothers. Their fathers were the first men they loved. And so, naturally, they measure their progress toward womanhood in their fathers' eyes. A father's interest, encouragement, and approval make a daughter feel she is doing things right. Your support gives your daughter confidence. Confidence, of course, is what makes her want to look ahead and plan her life with enthusiasm and purpose.

Women's childhood relationships with their fathers are important to them all their lives. Regardless of age or status, women who seem clearest about their goals and most satisfied with their lives and personal and family relationships usually remember that their fathers enjoyed them and were actively interested in their development.

Five sisters each described their father, separately, in almost the same terms: as a lonely but brilliant man who was very hard to be close to. In spite of that, each of them had a very special relationship with him. He had encouraged them from the time they were very small children to share his hobbies and intellectual interests. Each one remembered being flattered at the opportunity. Each sister picked the interest that suited her best and staked out territorial rights. Working, talking, learning, and watching him, they all got to know him at his concerned, patient, sensitive best. Each felt he knew and appreciated her as she was. They knew his shortcomings and sometimes suffered from them. But the love and care and interest he gave them through their growing years, in the best way he could, had a lasting positive influence on them as adults.

They haven't all continued with his hobbies or interests, but they all have professional careers and extracurricular interests. These daughters pursue their work with almost the seriousness their father does. However, fathers aren't the only influence on girls. The sisters are more relaxed about life than their father is. They learned that from their mother, perhaps, who interrupted her career for fifteen years to enjoy them and watch them grow.

Fathers, like mothers, are individuals first and parents later. Each father has to find his own path to parenthood. Men cannot all be playmates, coaches, teachers, comforters, confidants, mentors, or heroes to all their daughters all the time.

Some fathers (like mothers) get along best with babies. Some are more interested in girls when they are in their teens. Nine to twelve, however, is the age when fathers may be most appreciated. This age, with its intense enthusiasm, is a time when girls love friends and relatives *almost* as much as they love horses. Their devotion can be irresistible. As differences between fathers' and mothers' roles become less distinct, more and more fathers are discovering this to their pleasure.

Fathers don't have to have a PROGRAM. There's no formula. Fatherhood is just like friendship. It develops easily in simple ways.

Notice your daughter's friends. Know them apart. If you haven't seen one for a while, ask about her. Surprise your daughter now and then in small ways. One of the women we talked with still has a matchbox collection her father started for her when she was ten, bringing back additions from every trip he took until he died. Another father worked on stamps with his daughter. Another helped his daughter with math every night during seventh grade until he finally convinced her that she could master it as well as her brother.

Don't be afraid to ask questions. At this age all you have to do is ask one and sit back and listen. Let your daughter know *you*, too. Talk about your work, tell her tales of your childhood.

Fathers can seem powerful and overwhelming to their daughters. Let her see your soft side. Express your feelings and reactions. Tell her where you came from and how you got here. Let her see that you have had fears, failures, anxious times, hurts, just like hers, even though you may look flawless to her.

Share your good moments. Don't hide your pride in your achievements. Let her know that success is *possible,* if not inevitable or essential, and fun, too.

Enjoy her girlishness. Appreciating her person helps her develop confidence in herself just as much as enjoying her ideas and helping with her plans and admiring her achievements.

The object of feminism is to expand women's lives—not to make women carbon copies of men. If you want your daughter to grow up free to choose her own role as a woman, make sure she has the same encouragement to develop and the same advantages and opportunities to explore

114

that her brother has. Don't let her feel that it's unfeminine to make plans, work for goals, and be ambitious.

Take what's important to her seriously. If she gets A's in school, pay attention. Don't take good work for granted as if it were another aspect of the pleasing, obedient, diligent image a girl is supposed to present in public.

Take her problems seriously. We often consult with parents about children's school troubles. John came because he could not read, at eight. His parents were anxious about whether it would handicap him academically, whether he would get over it, whether it would interfere with his chances in life. When we see a child who has a problem, we always ask about the siblings, since learning problems run in families. We saw John's older sister, Amy, ten. She was a non-reader, too, a year behind her age mates in school and still barely passing. Her parents knew this but they didn't think it was a problem for Amy. Although she was brighter than her brother, it never occurred to her parents that she might like to have a career or simply get an education.

Give your daughter equal attention, equal care, equal opportunities. Give equal responsibilities, too. Don't excuse poor work habits, laziness, irresponsibility because "girls don't have to know that" or "Sally isn't as durable as you are, Jim." Don't let her brother do her chores because "a girl shouldn't have to clean up a mess like that."

Set standards and have expectations for her as you do for her brother—to suit her age, abilities, schedule, and temperament. Don't excuse her or favor her. That is just as damaging to her self-esteem and confidence as denying her opportunities or failing to treat her seriously.

Even at this age girls recognize when they are being favored for being girls. One child told us her father criticized her mother for spoiling her. "She bawled my brother out for teasing me, but I'd made fun of him first. My father was right." That girl appreciated the fact that her father expected her to follow the same standards of behavior that her brother did. She appreciated his serious attention.

Sex Education—Explicit and Indirect

One modern mother we know prepared her twelve-year-old for camp by telling her about menstruation, supplying her with the proper equipment in case her periods started, and then advising her, matter-of-factly, how to avoid pregnancy.

The daughter sent back an ecstatic account of camp life and the horses a few days later, ending: "P.S. I'm not pregnant yet." Her parents didn't appreciate the postscript until they arrived at camp for visitors' weekend and saw the boys. Beside the girls, they looked like eight-year-olds.

Girls at this age aren't usually interested in boys because the boys they know are, in their vocabulary, "babies." But while girls are not usually practicing sex at twelve, they're certainly thinking about it, and sometimes worrying about it. They're thinking about whether they're attractive. They're wondering whether they have to act differently with boys, now, and how to act. They're worried about whether boys will like them as much as they'll like boys.

They need encouragement. Fathers' criticism is more devastating than mothers' for reasons we have just been exploring. "Build, don't batter" is a good guideline for both parents. If you don't like the way your daughter has put herself together when you meet for breakfast, try to grin and ignore it, unless it becomes a habit. Praise what you can. Overlook what you can't.

We all bring from our childhood families habits and reactions that don't suit the moment. Try to become aware of them. It's a good first step toward uprooting them. Did your mother ever say, "Boys don't like girls who talk too much"? Did your father ever say, "You're too smart for a girl. You don't have to have all the answers," or "Try not to talk so much. Boys like to talk about themselves"?

Remarks like that make girls feel that the way they are is the wrong way. Then they begin to be afraid. They start to worry about how to make themselves popular, attractive, and "normal." They lose touch with their real selves. In changing to please boys they begin to fake and they end up in fake relationships that can't make either partner happy.

What is good sex education? First, it's accurate information about male and female physiology, reproduction, sexual intercourse, birth control, venereal disease. It's an important part of the preparation for a happy sex life. It's as vital for a girl's protection as the immunizations that she got in early childhood. She should get sex education in the same routine fashion. Some parents can teach it themselves, starting when daughters are very small.

Perhaps when she was a three-year-old your little girl noticed blood on your sheets or clothing and asked spontaneously what happened.

Hopefully, your answer was simple and direct. "It's blood. Mommy bleeds every month." That's all.

Later, perhaps, you asked her to get you a sanitary pad. Naturally she asked what it was. Naturally you told her that it protects your clothing when you are bleeding. That's all. Then you waited for questions. They were your clues to what she wanted to know.

Again, when she was old enough to read and help you shop, she fetched the sanitary materials one day, read the label, and, as if she'd never heard before, asked all over again, "What is this stuff?" You gave a fuller explanation of menstruation, relating it to reproduction, perhaps (see Chapter Eight on menstruation). Or her older friend got her

117

period. She told you and asked for more information, and so on and on.

You were careful from the beginning to answer truthfully and simply. You tried not to give her the idea that bleeding was a curse or a plague, an illness or a handicap. You didn't conceal the truth by saying that the blood she saw was to-mato juice or came from a scratch. Children have an un-canny ability to sense deception. It makes them wonder what you're hiding, and why. They imagine the worst. Then sex and being a girl become frightening.

If you have the knack for talking easily about what your body does, the whys and wherefores, you may be able to continue more intimate discussions of sex and sexual feel-ings right through puberty. However, parents and children often become diffident. Children have some embarrassment or shyness about revealing their most private questions, fan-tasies, and anxieties about sex to parents. They find it hard to imagine mothers and fathers as sexual beings. Parents, particularly fathers, have a somewhat similar problem deal-ing with the approaching womanhood of their "little" girls.

The sex or human relations course in school or the dis-cussion group in the community center, church, or Y may be able to give the kind of information girls want, and should have, better than you can. The only danger is that in the classroom sex may become another subject, with a life of its own. Unless the course and its leader are superior your child will memorize the facts, get a mark, and go away with the basic questions unasked:

How can I be close to another human being? How can I make him happy? How can I be happy with him? What do we need to make a relationship last?

She may never ask these questions of you, either. But, even if you never discuss them directly, her life with you through her childhood will influence the answers she finds.

The self-confident person comfortable with herself and her body, able to give and enjoy affection, sensitive, tender and kind, honest, true, and loyal is well prepared for satisfying, deep adult relations. Of course, these qualities come partly from temperament, but they are largely learned from the example and care of parents.

Your daughter's satisfaction with herself and her body began, perhaps, with the pleasure she saw in you as you bathed and dressed her, and watched and played with her as a baby. It grew with the sweet pats you gave her irresistible round bottom, the hugs and kisses just because you loved her, the amused smiles as you watched her find her own pleasant places—thumb, hair, ears, toes, vagina, navel, clitoris—your acceptance of her natural curiosity about sex when she played the exploring games of kindergarten.

Children become affectionate from seeing and feeling affection. When parents pat, hug, and kiss each other, and tickle, touch, and fondle their children, children pat, hug, and kiss back. They express and respond to affection easily. When they get old enough to feel sexual stirrings they're not awkward and uncomfortable. They aren't afraid that they'll be overwhelmed if they show their feelings.

Children learn to respect themselves and their feelings and judgment and to respect other people because they were raised with respect. When they're not pushed against their grain to go to dancing school when they don't like it, or be an athlete when they're not, or be smarter or more charming than they can be—when they're loved, as is—they gradually like themselves *as is*. Self-confidence helps give them judgment about other people, makes them wise in their choice of friends.

Kindness, tenderness, honesty, loyalty come from seeing, feeling, and imitating. Friendship is learned by watching and listening to you. If she sees that your friends are people you like and trust and don't pretend with—people who suit you—she probably won't pick friends who just pass by, or people who can help her or improve her status.

If you treat friends in a special way, if you are kinder, more generous, more sympathetic, more forgiving with friends, she probably will be, too.

What more can you do? Nothing. Except to remember as always that each child is a separate person, yours, forever, but *never* fully yours. She can never be all you wished or wanted, or all you know she could be. But she will be a better human being if you can let her be herself.

Q. Is self-consciousness common at this point in development? What can we do to overcome it?

A. Self-consciousness is no more common at this age than at any other. However, the girl who develops ahead of, or later than, her friends may be a bit uncomfortable about being different. The early-to-mature may insist on wearing the drabbest, most shapeless clothes, just when you would think she'd be proud of her new figure. The late bloomer may feel completely left out and go into temporary seclusion. This self-consciousness is *very* transient. There's nothing you can do to help. The less attention you call to it, the better. You may be mildly reassuring to the girl with budding breasts if you say something casual like "Why don't you wear that lovely blue T shirt? You look so nice in it." But if your daughter resists your suggestions or ignores them, don't push! Avoid making an issue of appearance. You'll simply underscore your daughter's dissatisfaction with herself. Then the self-consciousness may become fixed.

Q. I have a friend whose daughter was so conscientious she could never stop working on her homework. When ordered to bed, she couldn't sleep. Is this normal?

A. Conscientiousness can get out of hand at this age. Often teachers lay on the work when they get worried about whether their sixth graders will be prepared for junior high. Their warnings and the sometimes suddenly increasing difficulty of the work can make the conscientious child go overboard. What to do:

121

1. Put a limit on study time. Go over homework with your daughter. Help her plan how much time to give each subject and don't let her exceed it. She may get very upset. But if you insist, she'll generally find she can live with the restriction—in fact, do as well as or better than when she was behaving like a workaholic. A parallel case: compulsive packers finally stop packing, unpacking, and rearranging belongings when someone says, "You'll miss the plane."

2. Ask around. See if the teacher is revving the kids up a bit too much. If so, get together with a few other mothers for a quiet talk with her. (Keep your daughter out of it.)

3. Look at the family and classroom picture. Has a competitive sibling just had a big success? Has a new child who threatens her supremacy entered her class? Have you been having any disturbing family problems? If there is a stressful situation in her life at the moment, try to reason with her about it.

4. If your efforts to control her work habits seem to make things worse, you may have a problem. If work is edging out social life, friendship, and participation in family affairs, and not bringing much reward anyway, it would be a good idea to get some advice from the school psychologist or your pediatrician.

Q. How can you help a girl who matures earlier or later than her peers?

A. Hold her hand. Remind her that it will pass. And it will, before you know it. All the peers will be on a par again, relatively speaking.

Q. My eleven-year-old daughter has gained a lot of weight recently. I don't want to make her self-conscious but I'd like to keep her from having a weight problem later, if I can. What do you suggest?

A. A sudden gain in weight at puberty is not usually permanent. Children often get pudgy just before their final growth spurt. Then the excess weight seems to redistribute itself like magic and they go back to the body structure that is normal for them. If you want, you might occasionally remind your daughter (perferably when brothers and sisters are not around to tease) that she really shouldn't have a second piece of cake, or the fourth piece of bread or second glass of milk. However, reminding can easily turn into unpleasant nagging. Children know that eating too much makes them fat. The time comes when they begin to care about how they look. Then they usually learn how to control their weight on their own.

A few general words about *overweight in children*. The time to establish good eating patterns is in the cradle. There is some evidence that children who are stuffed when they're babies and toddlers develop larger-than-normal fat cells, which predispose them to eat more and metabolize fat less efficiently, and thus develop a chronic weight problem. There is no particular advantage in giving your baby as much as she can eat or working for faster weight gain than normal. Don't force her to drink a whole quart of milk a day. Also, TV and the casual life we lead have had an insidious effect on our diet. People snack too much and eat too little. The result: families don't eat meals together; children eat all the time. It's easy to lose track of what or how much nourishment they're getting.

Mealtimes are often the only times families are together. They provide a rare opportunity for parents to keep track of what's going on and to communicate the messages they think are important. They also establish good nutritional standards. Try to nourish your children, physically and mentally and emotionally, at meals. Put strict limits on

123

snacking between meals, and you may avoid a lot of problems, besides overweight.

Q. Some mothers in my daughter's class seem eager to push their children into dating and boy-girl parties at age ten. My daughter isn't ready and she feels left out. What can I do for her?

A. You can't make your daughter happy about being left out, but perhaps you can be happy yourself that she is being spared the excesses of parents who groom their ten-year-olds for the Popularity Crown. We can't overemphasize the disservice it is to little girls to make them feel that how they look, who likes them, where they're invited, and what people say about their charms are matters of importance—particularly at this very tender formative age.

Whatever you or your daughter may think, most girls feel inadequate to cope with dating, pleasing boys, and getting along with boys at this age, and boys feel the same way. Pushing them by making them think boy-girl socializing is expected increases their sense of inadequacy and may have long-range negative effects on their feelings about themselves and their ability to judge boys, choose friends appropriately, and relate happily to boys.

Your best line is to reassure your daughter that she'll do just fine. She may not believe it now, but she'll find out. Don't push. Don't worry. She can't be the only girl or boy in this predicament. Encourage appropriate social activities. Take an interest in her interests and ride it out.

Q. I feel my husband spoils our daughter. He thinks I'm too strict. How can we resolve this?

A. If you mean by spoiling that he pays too much attention to her, or helps her too much, be grateful. Most fathers help too little. If you mean he countermands your disciplinary measures or demands for help or the standards you set, maybe you should talk this over together. He shouldn't in effect undermine your authority with your child. On the other hand, perhaps you're asking too much. Review.

Sometimes mothers—particularly mothers who missed the attention from their fathers that their husbands seem to lavish on their daughters—have a little unacknowledged jealousy of their children. It's natural, but silly. If you feel you get less attention than your daughter, don't be ashamed to say so. Don't be a martyr. Ask for special time for yourself. It's much better than interfering with the father-daughter relationship.

Finally, there is nothing wrong with parents having different standards of discipline and performance. Children learn to accommodate to their fathers' and mothers' differing expectations. What upsets them is when parents fight out their disagreements through their children.

Q. My parents made me wear frilly clothes, complained when I wanted to play baseball with boys, ignored my desire to be a scientist. We've given our daughter freedom. She has riding lessons, music lessons, tennis camp, dancing, summer classes in language and anthropology—anything she's interested in. She's stopped studying, only getting B's when she could get A—. We're afraid when she wakes up and wants to be someone it will be too late. How can we persuade her?

A. Let her alone and cut out half or three fourths of her extracurricular program. In your efforts to provide the freedom you felt you missed, you have strait-jacketed her life so that she couldn't possibly have time or energy to think about what *she* might want to do. Freedom is the right to decide for yourself. You are deciding to make your daughter fill your frustrated dreams.

125

CHAPTER SEVEN

Adolescence

Thirteen to Seventeen

Children used to be children. Then they became adults. Now, for an ever-lengthening interlude, they are adolescents.

Earlier societies helped children pass smoothly into adulthood. Boys and girls were assigned well-defined adult roles early in life. They learned their parents' work, chore by chore, beside them. They grew into adult roles and responsibilities as they grew up to them.

Nowadays most children don't even know what their parents do outside the family. As the world has become more complex, the training needed for adult survival and success has become more sophisticated and demanding. It takes longer and longer for boys and girls who have passed childhood to get ready to be on their own.

Adolescence is a period during which physically, mentally, and sexually mature young people remain dependent on their parents while they prepare to make their adult way alone.

That is the crux of the so-called adolescent problem.

Fathers and mothers today have almost sole responsibility for their children's healthy development and success. Even if *their* parents are available and willing to help, they aren't able. The world has changed so fast in one generation that there really *is* no voice of experience. Today's fathers and mothers—with only the American dream for guidance—extend and overextend themselves, physically, emotionally, and financially, during the best years of their lives to ensure that their children will grow up prepared to do better and go further than they did.

As their best years grow shorter they understandably look to their children to justify the compromises, the deferred dreams, the abandoned goals. By the terms of their unwritten contracts, the children are supposed to prove it was all worth while.

Adolescents aren't usually up to it.

They want freedom now, but they're afraid of it. They want to control their lives, but, given carte blanche to choose the career that is most fulfilling, they panic. They haven't enough life experience to know what they want. They haven't enough maturity to wait, work, and worry doggedly through the long years of preparation to find out whether they've chosen correctly.

Their situation makes it harder. It's as if the *things* parents shower on children from birth, the advantages they provide, obligate adolescents to repay in kind: to choose right, to prove worthy. Uncertain, to begin with, they feel compelled to choose the paths that unspoken family goals dictate, rather than *freely*. In this bind they feel like puppets, manipulated by their parents.

Powerful sexual urges, well-nourished intellects, and surging physical strength drive them to assert their independence. But their will to independence exceeds their capacity for it. And even their will is unreliable.

Feelings of competence, confidence, and strength are as erratic as hormone production during these years. Adolescents may be, almost simultaneously, overconfident and riddled with fear. They are afraid of their overpowering feelings, of losing control, of helplessness, of failure. Sometimes they act bold, to counteract their imperious yearnings to remain children. They are impulsive, impetuous, moody, disagreeable, overdemanding, underappreciative. If you don't understand them, remember, they don't understand themselves most of the time. They are unpredictable in behavior, achievement, interest, ability.

Their desire and their recognized responsibility to grow up and become independent in the face of doubts and fears force them to strike extreme postures. They're hostile. They withdraw. They ridicule you. They try by these childish methods to shake you off, distance themselves, until they can be yours and not yours—independent and still family.

They throw themselves on their peers—any peers, it sometimes seems—for warmth in the newness of their "unchildness." They have to live by the law of their generation, with whom they must get along for the rest of their lives.

They can long for your help but feel too vulnerable to ask. They may resist rescue even when they appear to be drowning.

If parents measure their success by their children's day-to-day performance during these years, they are bound to be disappointed. The bigger their investment in the child, and the more "adolescent" the adolescent, the greater the risk of tension and conflict and full-scale intergenerational war.

The prevailing myth of adolescence makes things worse. The media's insatiable appetite for drama, shock, news, nourishes it. Parents, under the influence of this myth and anxious, anyway, lose their perspective. They begin to mistake the myth for their flesh-and-blood child. Minor becomes major. Average becomes subnormal. Nothing is trivial enough to overlook. One false step and the teen-ager is under the microscope for intensive examination. Sexual irregularity, promiscuity, alcoholism, drug addiction, emotional breakdown, petty larceny—whatever has been hitting the headlines—may be suspected.

Teen-agers themselves are tempted to become the myth. It's easier than establishing one's own identity. As one twelve-year-old confided, "This is probably the best year of my life. Next year my parents are going to hate me."

The human personality has an almost infinite capacity for reorganization and change, and at no time in life is this more true. Young people of high school age can actually feel themselves changing. Progress is almost tangible. It's exciting. It stimulates more progress. Nevertheless, growth is not constant and smooth. Erik Erikson quotes an aphorism to describe the formless forming of it: "I ain't what I ought to be. I ain't what I'm going to be, but I'm not what I was."

"The promise of finding oneself, and the threat of losing oneself," as he says, can almost coexist.

Many children grow through adolescence with no ripples whatever and land smoothly and predictably in the adult world with both feet on the ground.

Some who have stumbled and bumbled through childhood suddenly burst into bloom.

Most shake, steady themselves, zigzag, fight, retreat, pick up, take new bearings, and finally find their own true balance.

During this vulnerable period, despite their exaggerated dependence on their peers, adolescents still need their parents' guidance and support. Whether you react to the myth or the child before you will make a tremendous difference. Adolescents usually grow up all right unless, under the influence of the myth, you freeze them into their lesser moments.

᛫ Teen-agers aren't children. They know they can't keep crying to Mommy when they're hurt. They recognize that failure, now, is for real. Fail a course, it's on your college record. Flub the SAT's, there's no real second chance. Careless drivers can kill. Careless lovers get pregnant. Careless pranks can end in jail.

You're not a child. Okay. But they treat you like one when they want to, all those grownups. They tell you what to wear. They make you eat more when you want to get thin. They make you eat less when you're starving. They criticize your friends and say they're no good. They put their feet down and say, "You can't go there," "You can't stay that late," "You can't go with them," "You can't have the car" . . . the course, the college, the summer job, whatever. . . .

They make you feel like children, when you know you have to grow up. They knock the pins out from under your self-confidence. They don't give you a chance to practice being responsible, deciding for yourself, trying to see what suits you, who you want to be.

That's a reasonable facsimile of how parents look and feel to teen-agers.

A certain amount of adolescent discomfort is inevitable. Parents can't possibly let teen-agers lead their own lives on their own. There is, however, a big area of discretion between too much and too little parenting. Adolescents have to feel that they are growing in mastery, responsibility, and

131

judgment if they are ever to develop and find their identity as adults.

Try to find the way to protect them where they need protection, and let them stand alone wherever they can. This will help them get and keep their bearings through this last important stage of growing up.

Decide what parts of their lives they should and can manage for themselves. Then hands off, even if they do make mistakes. Their mistakes will help them learn, and help them learn to assume responsibility for their actions.

Academic performance is their responsibility, plainly, by high school. Keep out unless you're asked to come in. By age thirteen children no longer have to be reminded that they won't get into college unless they get good marks and they won't get good marks unless they study. If they haven't learned, let the school handle the problem. If you are worried, worry with the school, not the children. Follow the school's advice as long as it makes sense. If it doesn't, consult a qualified expert.

Don't *ignore* schoolwork. Praise where praise is due, show concern when necessary. But *stay out of the act*. Don't tie gifts, favors, or privileges to performance. Don't sit on children to make them study. Help when requested. Make it clear that you expect them to carry out their assignments just as you carry out yours.

Respect them and your influence enough to let them alone while they develop taste in dress, appearance, style, and friends. Unless you both feel you have clear evidence that your child is being led badly astray by others whose immoral and malevolent influence she, in her innocence, cannot appreciate—keep out.

If you can't contain yourself, try to say your piece about her clothes, eye shadow, mascara, diet, or hairdo as coolly as you can, then drop it.

In our experience, teen-agers' experiments end faster when parents take them with a large grain of salt.

Don't put your daughter in the position of having to defend friends, behavior, and values. Teen-agers don't usually kick over the traces permanently. Past experience and training generally assert themselves in time. Let your daughter have the satisfaction of experimenting and making up her mind for herself. That's how she develops confidence in her judgment.

Give adolescents a role in the family. This will be easier than it used to be when mothers stayed home and ran the house and the children, and fathers went to work and shoveled snow. Certainly every working family and most families where women work at home have jobs for children. Household chores used to be assigned by sex. Now they're assumed by choice, quite commonly. A wife loves to iron and hates to cook. A husband loves to cook and hates to clean. A boy loves to do bathrooms because he likes to see them shine when he's finished. A daughter likes being responsible for the dog—walking, feeding, grooming, working (loving, too). Many parents pay children for helping. It's all wrong, in our opinion. There's little enough in our helter-skelter days and lives to make us feel that the family is our gang, our haven to feel close and warm in. Doing for each other is one way we feel together. Paying children to dump the garbage is like paying them to go to school or making them pay you for room and board.

Teach them to be responsible for money. You probably started them with an allowance for comics and baseball cards and treats when they were five or six. By thirteen they're ready for a BIG allowance. But don't give them an annual income and ask them to plan a total budget right off. Start simply. You might give a certain weekly amount for essentials—lunch and carfare and a separate sum for birthday presents, personal pleasure. If you include money for clothes, limit items included to incidentals at first, like stockings, underwear, sweaters, blouses, costume jewelry.

Decide together what the allowance is for. Settle on a figure that you both find reasonable. Then make clear that the allowance has to last—no extras, no loans. Don't be *too* tough for the first weeks. Then make the rules stick. Otherwise, nothing is learned.

Increase the responsibility as your daughter learns to manage. By senior year in high school, or even sooner, most girls can manage a checking account, plan ahead, and manage to buy what they need throughout the year without calling for help.

There are always exceptions. CB radios are the latest piece of indispensable teen-age equipment in some suburban communities. Before that it was the ten-speed bicycle or the $300 skis. Some parents recoil in shock at such lavish expenditures for teen-agers, who are "still children." That's their privilege. Teen-agers may complain, "Look what you spend on Florida, the tennis club, parties." Your answer is simple. We earn the money we spend. If you want expensive cameras, skis, boots, rackets, radios, hi-fi, you earn the money for it.

If you're all that rich you may agree to providing a matching grant if the item is huge. If you're not, don't sacrifice. Your daughter will like the skis, camera, or sailboat much better if she earns it. She may find after ninety hours of baby-sitting that the item she was saving for isn't worth it and switch her sights to a new tennis racket or clarinet. But see what working for her prize has done. It's made her exercise her judgment. It's made her think about what she *really* wants. And it's given her the right to choose, self-control, and a bit of power.

Help her find summer jobs that are worth doing if you

134

possibly can. Work is almost more important than the money earned. The experience and responsibility can counteract that awful helpless, parasitic feeling that so many adolescents get when they're fifteen, waiting to be twenty-five.

Some boys and girls are very "maternal." They are affectionate, patient, sensitive, and understanding with younger children. They can do things with handicapped or disturbed children that many adults can't, just because they are closer in size and experience. They're great tutors and often learn as much as they teach. They become stronger being protectors, comforters, and teachers to those even more frail than themselves. Work helps overcome their sense of being "useless" (their word) adolescents.

They can work in labs. They can work in hospital wards. They can help in libraries, playgrounds, state parks, camps, stores.

If they can't get jobs, they can take courses that aren't available in school—courses that give them a chance to explore subjects and careers that may help them find where they want to go. There's photography, potting, drama, sculpture, graphics, music, video, journalism, poetry, cooking, carpentry, auto repair. Typing and shorthand are useful skills for schoolwork and to help earn one's way through college.

At first girls have an advantage in adolescence. They get there sooner. They mature earlier. Look at any class of first- or second-year high school students. Many of the girls are as tall, as rounded as they ever will be. They move with smoothness and grace. They act as if they know what they are about.

Biology makes girls more mature at this age, but training plays an important role, too. If they've learned their lessons diligently, by adolescence they have a head start in the development of the skills that help in learning. They have an

135

easier time paying attention, listening to directions, getting down to work, and concentrating on it till they're finished.

Boys mature later, physically and sexually. Their training accentuates this developmental lag. In many families, brothers and sisters learn the same rules and are held to the same standards and values. But our culture encourages boys to model themselves in the image of the bold, brave, independent male who's going to manage the world.

Parents and teachers don't say, "He's a real boy" as much as they used to. But there's a note of indulgence in the way they scold the little boy, who doesn't mind. It tells boys that they probably should be independent and a bit unruly.

This may help explain why boys have more learning and emotional problems than their sisters in the thirteen-to-seventeen period.

It may also help explain why girls lose their early academic lead in high school. The training that makes them diligent, conscientious, and compliant little girls actually handicaps them for advanced academic work.

To find out who you really are, what and who you want to be, to choose your life work, your friends, and your close and intimate partner, you have to be able to open yourself to the world—to feelings, experience. You have to be able to experiment, adventure, follow beckoning paths, turn back easily when you don't like where you're going, be willing to fail. You need to recognize that perfection, the ideal, exists only in the mind, and learn to compromise without caving in or withdrawing. You need boldness, courage, imagination, assertiveness—the qualities that boys are licensed to develop and girls are implicitly taught to repress.

Boys spend their teen years slowly getting focused, surveying the terrain ahead, examining the paths they have to choose from to find the way to be an independent adult.

Girls have had it all laid out for them from early childhood.

In adolescence they settle into adult roles that they practiced even in play. In all kinds of ways—subtle, subliminal, and quite obvious—our culture encourages them to look on marriage and motherhood as their ultimate goal. They are taught to mold themselves for man.

While boys are learning to find themselves in adolescence, girls learn to find a man. Finding a man and finding yourself are incompatible goals, so lots of girls stop growing. This is reflected and has been measured in girls' academic decline in adolescence, in their loss of interest in science and other so-called masculine fields that require dedication, determination, and competition. Girls' development starts earlier than boys' and it stops earlier.

Bringing up girls this way today is as unrealistic as keeping a mule in a city apartment to carry home the groceries. No matter how much we may want our girls to be full-time wives and mothers when they grow up, and our sons to be strong, silent supporters of dependent women, times have changed. It just isn't like that any more in most families.

Nowadays the average family needs a wife's pay check to survive. Only 40 per cent of the nation's jobs, the Bureau of Labor Statistics reports, pay enough to support a family of four adequately. More than half the mothers of school-age children are at work. The vast majority are not ardent women's libbers, trying to escape their children. They're good mothers who work to provide what good mothers have been taught that children need: food, clothing, housing, and the start in life that prepares them to be responsible parents to their families, in turn.

Boys and girls are more alike than different. Training has maximized the differences. It has handicapped girls mentally and emotionally just as much as binding girl babies' feet crippled them physically.

It is realistic today for girls to anticipate lifelong employment just like their brothers, and they should prepare for it. Instead of fostering compliance and passivity and dependency, parents should encourage initiative, assertiveness, and independence. Then girls will grow up with the same expectations, goals, and responsibility about themselves and others as their brothers. Today's boys and girls will marry as equal partners. Shared responsibility, involvement, and commitment and more mutual interests may give marriage and the family more solid foundations than they have today.

Even if your daughter acts as if you're an ogre, she is exquisitely sensitive to what you think, say, do, and even *feel* about what she is and what she should become. It is therefore important to make your influence positive.

When our children started school, very few of their friends had mothers who worked. Your children may have few friends whose mothers stay home. But, while the two-job family is fast becoming the norm, bringing enormous changes in what mommies and daddies do, rules have changed faster than attitudes about what's masculine and what's feminine. People cling to their familiar ways of thinking, feeling, and seeing themselves and each other long after they have changed their ways.

Today's parents, whether they know it or not, are probably all guilty to a greater or lesser degree of giving their daughters the same messages that their parents gave them about what daughters ought to be. Making yourself aware of how you feel and react may help you act more appropriately.

Fathers First!

Many men still think that educating daughters is irrelevant. If there's not enough money for two children to go to college, boys go and girls, no matter what their promise, go to work or get married.

If a girl is strong-minded enough, she might borrow money, get a job, and go away to college on her own. She is not likely, however, to escape the effects of her father's rejection.

One young woman floated from major to major and man to man for a decade. *The diagnosis was clear.* She couldn't settle down to becoming a serious student with long-range goals for fear her achievement—or lack of it—would confirm her father's judgment of her worth. She couldn't settle down with a man for fear he'd push her around the way her father did if she allowed herself to become attached to him, to get too close.

Another girl got a large scholarship to a first-rate college. Her father said he couldn't afford to pay the balance. He felt that the city university was good enough. Her gesture of independence was to get married. Two children and thirteen years later she is divorced, working, and going to college at night to get where she might have been at twenty-one.

Happy, bright, nubile daughters are enchanting. Fathers often relapse into a kind of teen-age helplessness in their presence. Then the daughter who comes for help with a math problem may hear things like "Don't move. Let me look at you," or "Why worry about math? You can always smile."

Fathers mean to tell their daughters how much they love and admire them. They don't realize that daughters hear a

139

different message: "You're lovely to look at. You're desirable. That's all that matters. Don't be serious."

Girls are, variously, confused, puzzled, pleased, and flattered. In any case, they are distracted from their serious purpose. They begin to think of themselves as pleasure-giving objects. Their fathers' undifferentiated pleasure and delight make them think of themselves as cute-as-a-button things, whatever they do, or FAIL TO DO.

Success was unnecessary. PLEASING was ALL. Girls came to feel that there wasn't much purpose in whatever it was they might have thought they wanted to accomplish or strive for.

Their brothers would spend hours over college catalogues, or discussing careers with family friends in different businesses and professions. Fathers and brothers would talk at the dinner table: politics, space, computers, war and peace. Girls talked, too. Then, in the midst of finding words to express a complex idea, a girl might catch that smile that said, "Isn't she cute struggling over that big thought" on her father's face. She'd hear herself stuttering. She'd feel herself blush. She'd look helpless and giggle and give up.

Recently someone on radio asked Marian McPartland, the great jazz pianist, why there weren't more women in jazz. "It's hard," she said, "if you're playing some spot and you're trying to work your way to where you're going next. You're lost in the music—simply lost. You don't see anything going on. Your head's down. Your mouth may be hanging open. Your hair's in your face. Most women can't handle that. They're used to putting their faces together and recognizing people when they come in and all that. They have to be attractive. I had trouble for a long time."

It would be awful if fathers did not notice their daughters and appreciate their appearance and their charm. Girls need to be loved and feel loving in adolescence just as much as when they were little. It's one thing, however, to appreciate a daughter's looks and style, and let her know it, and quite another to make her feel that she's just a cuddly thing.

There *are* times when looks and social behavior are the relevant issue. It might be appropriate, for example, to admire a girl's dress, her poise, her ability to make other people comfortable at a dance, but quite belittling to interrupt her when she's making a difficult point in a serious discussion to tell her how cute she is. Can you imagine telling a teen-age boy he looked cute when he kicked the winning goal in a football game?

Men don't usually set out to denigrate their daughters in these ways. They repeat, unconsciously, the kinds of behavioral patterns—tics, almost—they learned from their fathers. It would be better if they made a conscious effort to adjust to the times. If they put down daughters in this innocent fashion, they probably behave the same way with their wives. Thus girls learn twice that, in men's eyes at least, they are inferior; that they are for fun, for sex, and not to be taken seriously.

It's warm and funny and loving when a man is so overcome with sexy feeling for his wife that he pretends he didn't hear the question she asked him. But if none of her serious questions ever gets answered it's a clear put-down.

A sign of the times is the growing number of middle-aged, middle-class women who have diligently gone back to school, gotten their credentials, and finally found jobs that interest them.

A matching sign of the times is their husbands' reactions. For every man who boasts of his wife's hard work and success, there are dozens who can't help putting the whole effort down. The remarks are so frequent they're fast becoming clichés: "We hope she'll be able to pay for the maid before she retires." "She shoved me into the next tax bracket." "She's more expensive to keep since she got her job."

It's always very jolly, with most of the wives joining in the fun. They can afford to. At their age the chance to do what they like means more than power. Besides, they may be mature enough to recognize the anxiety men feel about losing the *image* of dominance that can sometimes cover up a trembling ego.

It may not be so amusing to adolescent daughters. For obvious reasons fathers' attitudes, the goals and values they encourage, are more influential than mothers'. We've found that women who have succeeded in men's fields with grace, confidence, and seriousness invariably had support from their fathers during their growing years. They were brought up to believe that normal women could still be people, with as much interest in expressing themselves, challenging their abilities, and getting ahead as their brothers had.

We found our impression scientifically documented in a recent report on a group of gifted women who have been studied since their early childhood in the twenties.[1] Those whose lives seem to have borne out the early promise they showed all mentioned their father's support as a prominent influence.

When fathers put down mothers they put down daughters, too. The put-down has a reverberating effect. Women who combine work, marriage, and motherhood constantly cope with ambivalent feelings about their femininity and their ambitions. The put-down brings these feelings to the surface. The anxiety, thus roused, often focuses on a daughter. The mother, through her attitudes and reactions, will pass on to her daughter her own conflict and confusion about how to be a woman.

Mothers' Influence

If you are a mother reading this book, you probably want your daughter to be free to decide how to live her life in a way you may never have experienced. You don't want her to slip into some old feminine stereotype. You feel she is valuable and important. You want her to grow up knowing you feel that way, knowing it in herself. You want her to be free to shape her own life instead of shaping herself to suit a husband who will then create her adult image.

But we carry the past in our hearts and minds as our mothers did before us. The roles we played in childhood and grew into as we grew up, with all the musts and no-nos that made them take, all the defenses and wiles we learned to help us adapt and adjust, are with us still—closer to the surface in some than in others.

Sometimes when we're not looking they all come out— voices from the past—giving our daughters crossed signals and false messages. Make yourself aware, and check them.

Beware the put-down. See it for what it is. Laugh it off. Don't let it stir up the old ambivalence. Don't let it shake your daughter's faith in herself, her goals for life, her femininity.

Hear yourself when you are talking in echoes. When you say things to a teen-ager like "Do people wear jeans on dates?" or "Don't you think you might try to make yourself look attractive?" recognize the voice as yesterday's. There is no fifty-item scale that tests a girl's femininity any more. There are as many ways to be feminine as there are women. Trust your daughter, if she has your confidence and support, to find her own self. Then style—where to part her hair, how to stand and walk, sit, dress—will fall into place to match.

We live in informal times. Girls and boys, men and women: all of us are allowed to relax and forget ourselves and concentrate on more important concerns than how we look from moment to moment.

The dreadful fears mothers used to instill in their daughters about being a wallflower, about not being "pinned," die hard. They stimulate thoughtless comments and criticism. They may make you blow hot and cold about ambition, enterprise, hard work. Step on them when they surface. Don't let them out. Don't encourage your daughter's ambition and achievement in one breath, then worry in the next when she refuses to spend weekends at the pizza parlor with the gang because she has a paper to finish, or finds all that "hacking around" a bore. Respect her feelings. If she wants to be a teen-age grind, remember it may make her a twenty-five-year-old success. Remember, too, that excess is as typical of adolescence as changeability. Let her study while she's in the mood.

Does she scream and shout? Argue like a political boss, flush with excitement at the battle? Does it make you nervous when she fights for her ideas? How does a person learn to be serious, involved, determined—all those things one often must be to achieve what one cares about?

Maybe it used to be "pushy" and inappropriate for girls to argue, contradict, persist—particularly with men. But that was when girls were taught "Don't talk about yourself." "Let boys do the talking." "Draw them out."

If you don't know what to tell your daughter in these days of transition when the lessons you learned don't fit, confess your confusion or keep quiet.

Watch out for hidden envy. Your daughter has many choices and opportunities that you did not. Try not to kill her joy in them by pushing her too hard to fulfill herself. Accept delirious adolescent binges as par for the course. She may bury herself in Tolstoy in May and become a potter in June. Perhaps her enthusiasms *are* shallow. Maybe serious people don't reach their goals in this hit-or-miss way. The important factor to note is the enthusiasm and dedication. Focus comes later.

Not all girls want to be Ph.D.'s or to star in exotic vocations hitherto barred to women. It may give you vicarious pleasure to watch your daughter constantly proving that girls can do anything boys can. But if what *you* want your daughter to do is not *her* choice, too, you are dictating. Dictating does not liberate, however noble its purpose. It is also counterproductive when practiced on adolescents.

The road from childhood to maturity is never straight. Young people get where they are going by daydreaming and fantasizing. They also test future roles by trying them on to see how they feel and fit.

The lighthearted, apparently empty-headed fourteen-year-old is not bound to dance her way through life, although playfulness will still be an attractive part of her nature when she does find what she wants to be and gets serious.

If you curb young people's efforts to get free just as they are trying freedom out, some give up trying to be responsible. Others get as stubborn as a five-year-old. Nag too much, criticize too much, and you actually force some girls to hang on to positions that would have been temporary way stations on the road to adulthood.

Children have an elemental urge to independence. They instinctively know that the experience they get on their own will help them when they need to be *completely* responsible for themselves later.

Balking when you push too hard or interfere too insistently may be their inefficient, maladaptive adolescent way of saying, "Get out of sight. I have to do it myself."

Girls will need even less direction than boys, these days. Their schools, their friends, the world they live in—all are pushing them to plan for careers rather than pick-up jobs, for later marriages and smaller families. It's the style of our times, the "in" thing for women, just as super-motherhood was in the forties and fifties.

Answer questions, supply information you know she wants, give opinions when requested, and let your daughter find *her* way to be a woman.

Parents' influence is more indirect than specific. What do you do? How do you like it? How do you get along? Your children are looking and listening. If you are satisfied with the way you've made your life—whether you are at home or at work, conventionally successful, or living modestly—you make it easier for your children to grow up. You look good to them. They tend to accept your goals as theirs; they accept your general goals for them as reasonable. They incorporate your attitudes. They tend to be optimistic, confident, enthusiastic about today and tomorrow.

Mothers' attitudes are particularly influential. Fathers can stimulate and encourage, but mothers are the model of what a girl *must* be, as she sees it from the perspective of childhood.

We can't all be happy, optimistic, successful, satisfied, capable of coping all or even part of the time. But there are ways to protect daughters from the full impact of our adult problems.

Mothers who project an image of helplessness and inability to cope, mothers who can't defend themselves from belittling husbands or unjust attack, have a terrifying effect on their daughters. Terrifying, because it corroborates all their adolescent fears about growing up, growing responsible, being successful. If mothers act like moderately successful grownups, then daughters know they can, too. If mothers have given up, daughters have a hard time imagining, through their adolescent trials and errors, that they can succeed.

Young children, in a recent study of the effects of divorce, recovered from their initial fear, anxiety, and loss of self-confidence—*often becoming confident and effective persons for the first time in their lives*—when their mothers went back to school for graduate training, went back to their abandoned careers, organized their social lives, got jobs. When mothers showed that they could cope, children relaxed, lost their anxiety, followed their mother models, and began to cope themselves.[2]

People who can't solve their problems not only are poor models, but often take out their failure and frustration on daughters. Working on your own problems is more productive than anxiously trying to perfect your daughter. Let teachers set academic standards. Let daughters be responsible for their work. Don't nit-pick. Try not to make every molehill into a mountain, every moment an occasion for improvement of speech, posture, manners, grammar, pronunciation, effort, or enterprise. If you are worried and anxious, try not to transmit that anxiety to your daughter by fussing anxiously. Make the time you spend with her positive. You may think you can protect her from having your problems as an adult by helping her to be perfect. But try to remember she is separate. She will grow confident from feeling your confidence. If you act as if you expected her to succeed, that expectation will become part of her. Growing up then just happens, from day to day: no bigger a problem than studying for the Friday math test.

147

QUESTIONS AND ANSWERS

Q. My daughter and her friends seem to worry about their weight constantly. They overeat, then go on crash diets. I wonder why, since none of them is fat to begin with. I have heard that this can lead to a very dangerous problem and would like some advice about persuading our child to be more sensible about herself.

A. You are probably referring to anorexia nervosa, which is a potentially fatal disorder. However, from what you say, you don't have to worry on that score.

First of all, your daughter and friends are typical of many teen-agers. Their attitude toward food and figure reflects the culture they were brought up in: almost every commercial on TV, it seems, encourages them to eat! The alternate ones urge them to try LOOZ, FAST, NOFOOD, to gain the model figure, without which total failure will be inevitable. Since teen-agers are growing fast, using up lots of energy, love to eat junk, and are very self-absorbed, you can see why the diet/stuff syndrome is a common one at this age.

Anorexia nervosa bears no more relation to this normal teen-age phenomenon than crying when hurt does to severe depression. Anorexia nervosa is a pathological condition. It is not common. The anorexic patient diets compulsively, but continues to believe she eats too much and is repulsively fat. If she does relax and eat a square meal or succumb to a sweet, she is likely to induce vomiting, or to exercise compulsively in a frenetic drive to burn up the calories consumed.

148

For diagnostic purposes, the anorexic is defined as a person who has lost one quarter of the body weight considered normal for age, height, and body structure, while still considering herself overweight. The body image is distorted. Other symptoms make it easy to distinguish anorexia from normal dieting. The anorexic tends to be withdrawn from family and friends and usually functions poorly in many areas.

The illness is psychogenic and there are different theories about the cause. The common thread is a fear of growing up and assuming the responsibilities of being a woman. Food may represent pleasure and be associated in the patient's mind with forbidden sex feelings that must be repressed. Dieting, in the confused mind of the anorexic, may represent an effort to avoid pregnancy. It may develop following a disastrous pregnancy of an older sister or cousin, or be related to unresolved childhood fears and wishes. It is a medical emergency and requires immediate attention.

There is not very much you can do about fad dieting, except try to discourage it and *encourage* normal eating habits and regular, enjoyable exercise as a more satisfactory and satisfying way to control weight. Girls will become less compulsive about their bust, waist, and hip measurements, we feel, as the move to change the sex-object view of women continues to gain momentum.

Q. Our local hospital has opened a special clinic for adolescents. Our daughter asked if she could leave the pediatrician who has taken care of all three of our children, and switch to the adolescent specialist. Can you explain the advantages, if any?

A. Adolescent medicine is a fairly new specialty. The doctors who practice it presumably have a particular interest in young people and their problems, both medical and emotional. The adolescent specialist offers the child, at this touchy, transitional period, the privacy that she often wants and needs.

Adolescents, in our opinion, should have an opportunity to leave their pediatricians—though many who have a comfortable, fond relationship with the doctor they've known since infancy won't want to. They should not be required to go to the family doctor, who may be and often is moralistic and unresponsive to their problems and needs.

The adolescent specialist will, for example, be prepared to treat incipient acne and decide when special dermatological care is required; treat menstrual disorders; consult about sex myths and fears; discuss issues relating to sex conduct; provide birth control advice and equipment; keep track of the adolescent's progress and, it is hoped, recognize and head off emotional problems before they become serious.

The adolescent specialist is particularly helpful for young people who cannot discuss at home their feelings about sex and their concerns about themselves—and their number is legion. Many parents feel uneasy about turning their fourteen- and fifteen-year-olds over to their own private doctor for fear this will shut them (the parents) off from knowledge they should have to give daughters the care, training, and protection they need. They are fearful that something might happen that they might have been able to prevent, if they had been informed. These concerns are understandable, but not very realistic. Perhaps if you have a clear agreement with your daughter and the doctor that you are to be told if and when there is a potentially serious problem, you will feel more comfortable about this generally successful branch of medicine.

Parents should obviously be told when a potentially serious medical problem develops, or when an emotional problem exists where their behavior might be influential, or their observation is important and necessary. And they must be told about a child's involvement in a dangerous or illegal activity.

NOTES

[1] Pauline S. Sears and Ann H. Barbee, School of Education and Department of Psychology, Stanford University, "Career and Life Satisfaction among Terman's Gifted Women," courtesy of the authors.

[2] Joan Kelly, Ph.D., and Judith Wallerstein, M.S.W., "The Effects of Parental Divorce," *American Journal of Orthopsychiatry,* Vol. 46, No. 1 (January 1976), pp. 20–32; No. 2 (April 1976), pp. 256–269.

❦ CHAPTER EIGHT ❦

Menstruation

Adolescents are creatures of their physiology. They are buffeted about by unseen, unknown forces conspiring within to change the body before the eyes, to stir up strange feelings and unpredictable responses at inopportune times. It's all very uneasy-making and it accounts for a lot of adolescent behavior—daring, ambitious, affectionate, dedicated, sensitive today; cringing, apathetic, cold, lazy, indifferent tomorrow.

Sexual maturity has a symbolic meaning that affects adolescents, too. It marks the chronological end of childhood. It signals the inevitability of growing up; becoming independent; finding sex, love, and success as man or woman. It poses a direct challenge to the self at the moment when the self may be most vulnerable.

Menstruation confronts girls with the reality of adulthood in a particularly undeniable way. Today, consciously at least, they know that the mythology of menstruation that fills the classical literature they have been studying since Sunday school is just that—mythology. They are not bound by the curse of Eve. They do not feel unclean. As the sanitary equipment ads say, "No one but you knows."

Certainly menstruation does not make girls feel weak, ill, crippled, or inferior to boys. Nevertheless, whatever they know about the facts of life, menstruation signifies unmistakably that they can now be impregnated and become mothers. They know that a mother is forever responsible for the child she brings forth.

In some parts of the world, even today, girls get a slap in the face for their first period and a harsh warning from their mothers, "Stay away from the boys now." But even without the warning they recognize their vulnerability. This fact can make their femininity itself a constant threat to their survival as people. The pleasure of sex is a threatening pleasure. They may have serious personal aspirations for study and work. They yearn to love and be loved. They fear ambition will cost them love, or that love will drain them of will and purpose and leave them helpless. Can they trust? Will they survive? Can they be both woman and person?

When girls are reasonably confident and sure of themselves, their anxieties come and go and the apparent dilemmas of adolescence are gradually more or less comfortably resolved. They develop plans and goals for their lives. They find compatible friends and lovers who answer their needs for companionship, affection, sexual expression, and closeness.

When they don't trust their abilities and their feelings, when they have a poor sense of themselves and their worth, the normal conflicts of adolescence can overwhelm them.

Some girls under these circumstances become wildly promiscuous. Learning how to be a person and express their femininity stimulates so much anxiety that they seem to give

154

up. Instead of learning to be themselves, and to make friends, they substitute sex for closeness. They use sex, like addicts, to make the problems of self go away.

Some develop anorexia nervosa, the psychogenic disorder with life-threatening consequences. They literally diet themselves into nothingness as if to say, "I won't eat, so I can't get pregnant." "My problems will shrink as I do." (See "Questions and Answers" at the end of Chapter Seven.)

At the other extreme, some defend themselves against their problems by eating too much. They substitute food for the forbidden fruit of sex. They defend themselves from love and its temptations with layers of fat that frighten off possible suitors—that make them feel armored against invaders.

They may put on sackcloth and ashes and seek seclusion. They bury themselves in their work; devote themselves to an ailing mother, an arcane religion, cults that dictate abstinence and impose rigid controls.

Some of these reactions are less common than they used to be, reflecting our more enlightened ways of raising girls. With less restriction in childhood and more encouragement to express their feelings and pursue their interests and ambitions, girls come to adolescence more comfortable about themselves and less ambivalent about their feelings and judgment.

Nevertheless, even the steady and sure can use some sensitive guidance from their mothers. It's not that they really believe any of those myths or old wives' tales about menstruation and sex and pregnancy and venereal disease. They probably do not ever consciously worry about how far they can go before they've gone too far to stop. They may worry less than you do about whether they'll damage themselves or their reputations by sexual behavior.

Still, they keep thinking weird thoughts:

155

Why don't I like the idea of having children? Am I going to have to let boys put their tongues in my mouth? Am I crazy to think it's repulsive? What will happen if I have intercourse? Won't it hurt? If I have a baby, how will I ever be the same? Am I strange, abnormal, not to like boys? Am I afraid? Why?

Very few adolescents—boys or girls—will spontaneously talk about thoughts like these with their parents. There is a natural reticence between parents and children of this age. Both are ill at ease with the fact of children's adulthood. Children, still insecure in their sexuality, are fearful of exposing themselves and zealous of privacy.

If you have answered your daughter's questions and talked about the basic processes of development and reproduction and the nature of her body, easily, as she grew, you may not find it too hard to open a dialogue again now. The fact that women have traditionally been freer to admit and express their feelings than men makes discussion between mothers and daughters easier than between fathers and sons.

But you must be sensitive in choosing the appropriate opening. Typically, a mother notices that her daughter is growing breasts and decides to PREPARE her for menstruation. She buys whatever sanitary products she thinks are suitable. She finds a private moment and slips them to her. Then a conversation like this ensues.

MOTHER: Mary Ellen, I want to talk about growing up.

MARY ELLEN (*bored*): Yeah, Mom. Judy already told me. Forget it.

or I've been getting periods for a year. Hadn't you noticed?

MOTHER (*relieved*): Well, if you ever have any questions, I'd—

156

MARY ELLEN: Sure, Mom. Thanks. I've got this algebra. I really have to get finished.

However *your* discussion begins, try not to let it end like that. Even if you are confident that your daughter is as well informed as you are—or better—remember you have more than facts to convey. Hopefully, you can help form her attitudes toward the sexual aspect of being female and share some of your feelings about being a woman. Your talks could even determine whether she grows up associating menstruation with pain and inferiority or treats it as a minor nuisance—inconsequential, in terms of its function in reproduction. We are not suggesting that you glamorize motherhood, or prescribe it for her, simply that you let her know again—as you have in many less direct ways—how *you* feel about being a mother, how it fits into the way you see yourself as a woman.

Unless you're relieved because you don't know where to go anyway (at the moment), dismiss the protests. Say something slightly silly like "Well, I've got to make my speech because I've been practicing it for years. I'll help you do your algebra when I've finished."

That should disarm her even if she really *does* know more than you do. If she really doesn't, she may secretly appreciate your enforced enlightenment.

Here is a version of what we would say. Cut, alter, amplify to suit.

"You probably know all about menstruation—what it is, what it's like, what it's for. I don't know where you found out or whether you really did get all your questions answered, but I'd like you to hear it again from me. Maybe I won't tell you anything new, but hearing me may make it easier for you to come back whenever you have questions or concerns about what's going on in your body, your feelings, or your mind, or when anything else in your life worries you."

Then explain what menstruation means—the female body maturing—as she knows it from the body changes she sees already. Tell her about body odors and vaginal secretions so she knows what to expect—what's normal. Tell her how to handle perspiration safely if she doesn't like the smell.

Describe menstruation itself. Here are the basic facts. At a certain point in development the ovaries and the pituitary glands begin to produce hormones that stimulate the ripening of one of the store of eggs that is present in the ovaries at birth. The mature egg is expelled from the ovary (ovulation). It travels through the fallopian tube to the uterus. While the egg has been ripening, the lining of the uterus has been building up under the influence of other hormones, to make it more receptive to the fertilized egg.

From approximately two days before the egg leaves the ovary until two or three days after it is expelled, conception is possible. If male sperm enters the fallopian tubes or uterus from the vagina, through intercourse and ejaculation, it can fertilize an egg that is already present. Sperm may also survive in the uterus or fallopian tubes long enough to fertilize an egg that is about to be released.

After conception, if pregnancy proceeds normally, the embryo (as the fertilized egg is called at this stage) attaches to the thick, nutritious lining that has built up in the uterus. As the baby grows, the point of implantation in the lining becomes the placenta. The developing child is nourished by the mother's blood system, through the placenta and the umbilicus, until birth.

If the egg is not fertilized, it slowly disintegrates. Levels of the hormones that build up the uterine lining drop. Blood vessel walls thin. Finally, approximately ten days after ovulation, menstruation begins. The menstrual flow washes away the unused lining so that a fresh one can build in preparation for possible conception in the following month.

Menstruation thus has a fundamental role in conception and reproduction.

We are not suggesting that you give an extended lecture like this. Elicit questions as you go. Try to recall your own adolescent questions and misconceptions. It may encourage your daughter to tell hers. Stop now and then to make sure she understands what you're telling her, and find out whether she has anything to say or ask.

Bring up the myths and misconceptions as well as the legitimate questions you can anticipate. Even when we dismiss myths and folk tales intellectually as baseless we don't quite shake off the message. They plant fears and misconceptions.

One way to introduce the subject is to ask her if she's ever heard any weird ideas or beliefs about menstruation and reproduction. If she doesn't think of any, suggest some. Has she ever heard menstruation called the curse? Does she know where that term comes from? Has she heard menstrual blood called "tears of the disappointed womb"? Does she remember the Bible stories in which menstruating women are called unclean and isolated from the community?

How can you explain the myths? Ask her to recall some of her own childhood fantasies about conception and birth. Did she think babies came out of the navel or were conceived by drinking male urine, for example? Recalling her own childish ideas will help her see why primitive people with very imprecise understanding of internal physiology based their explanations on what they saw. They associated blood with injury and illness. Since they could not know the cause of the blood "sickness" they were afraid. They avoided the menstruating woman for fear of being infected.

If a woman became ill for no reason, they may have seen it as punishment—for what? For her evil. There are, of course, other explanations for the primitive association of woman with evil. It suited men. It kept women subdued and submissive, discouraged them from straying. It may also have assuaged men's rage at women who rejected their love.

This might be a good point in the discussion to contrast the myths with reality. Describe normal menstruation. Here, for your own reference, are the basics.

Periods occur about every twenty-eight days, give or take a week.

Periods last about four to eight days—usually about five.

The average blood loss is about three ounces per period, though it may range normally from two to sixteen.

Blood loss, unless continuously excessive, is not harmful; does not cause anemia; does not tire, weaken, or handicap a woman. She can ride, play tennis, chop wood, do as she pleases. She may not want to swim on the first days when flow is more profuse, for purely aesthetic reasons. Whether or not a woman has sexual intercourse during menstruation is a matter of choice.

Sudden profuse flow may occur early in the period. If your daughter has this experience she may want to take the precaution of using extra protection at this time.

Painful periods are rare, although many young women do have pain before the period, or during the first day or so, in the first years of menstruation. Aspirin usually offers sufficient relief. If it doesn't, your daughter will let you know and you might want to give her an over-the-counter pain killer, or consult your doctor for advice.

There are many fewer complaints about pain than there used to be. Doctors attribute this to changes in girls' lives. They not only get more exercise and are better nourished; they have less fear and inhibition about menstruation and sex. They are more physically relaxed as well as less anxious.

Periods are apt to be irregular at first; the hormonal flow that regulates menstruation has to become established. Sometimes women stop menstruating, not because they are pregnant or ill, but because of an unexplained decline in hormone production. The condition is called amenorrhea. It seems to accompany severe physical and mental stress. It was common among women in the concentration camps in World War II. It may be nature's way of protecting the species by preventing the birth of inferior or endangered children.

A little cautionary advice: (1) Pick the right moment for your first talk with your daughter. A weekend afternoon or evening when the other children, if any, are away or busy outdoors, and father is not likely to interrupt, would be ideal. Make sure that you don't choose a time when your daughter is preoccupied with studying for a final examination or waiting for a call or visit from her best friend. (2) Try not to talk too long or too much—a common mistake when you are trying to put a person at ease and don't want to make her feel uncomfortable about having to comment or ask a question. You can encourage your child to talk by stopping now and then to make sure she understands, by asking *her* questions. Beyond giving her a lot of straightforward, factual information to clear up doubts and fears and misconceptions, you also want to convey sensitivity and warmth, and *not* clinical detachment. You want to leave your daughter with the feeling that you are a sensitive as well as sensible, dependable, and understanding person to confide in. You want to make her feel comfortable about sex and her own sexuality.

Do not feel bound by the outline or table of contents we have suggested for your discussion. You have to use *your* best judgment to reach *your* daughter most effectively. There is no possible way that we can prescribe or anticipate the most effective way to reach her without knowing you both. You have your own style, your own manner of bringing up things you want to talk about. You must know when to keep still, when to talk. You must have a fair idea of what particular subjects your daughter might want to discuss. These suggestions of ours are at best just that—a starting point to stimulate your own thinking, a guide to help you plan what you want to convey.

CHAPTER NINE

Sex Education for Parent and Child

Last summer two couples we'll call the Smiths and the Joneses rented a lakeside vacation cottage in Wisconsin.

After an early supper their daughters, Ellen and Jan, took off to explore the place. They didn't show up again until nearly midnight.

With male voices calling good-bys behind them, the girls came in and plopped on the floor, happy and exhausted.

"This place is the greatest," Ellen said. That was as far as they got. Four parents on the edge of their chairs faced them, grim and angry.

The Smiths and Joneses could have reacted in several ways. They chose the least effective and perhaps the most dangerous one. They didn't listen to the girls' report. They didn't ask questions. They ACCUSED!

The Pill has taken much of the fear out of sex. The new morality has minimized guilt about sex. Yet the sexual revolution has intensified, rather than allayed, parents' perennial anxiety about teen-agers.

Parents still fear that their inexperienced adolescents will get too deeply involved before they know what they are doing and realize the consequences. They are also afraid that the seductive influence of the new morality will turn their sons and daughters into virtuosos of promiscuity.

Parental anxiety is not always unfounded, but it is highly exaggerated. There *is* a new morality. It has changed sexual behavior for adolescents as well as for their parents. But it has not changed teen-agers' individual moral and human standards.

In the past few years we have had wide-ranging interviews on behavior and beliefs with ninety-one adolescents whom we have followed since infancy in the New York Longitudinal Study. What we learned about their views on sex and about their behavior confirms what other investigators of the contemporary adolescent scene have reported, and probably accurately reflects the morals and mores of today's middle-class adolescents.[1]

Today's teen-agers have much less guilt about sex than those of previous generations. Freedom from guilt, however, has not set off a mad rush into sexual activity. Moreover, the sexually active are no more casual or promiscuous today than yesterday.

A surprisingly low (in view of the popular stereotype of teen-age behavior) 10 per cent have sexual intercourse by the end of their junior year in high school. When they do, it is usually the culmination of a long and serious affectionate relationship. Emotional and physical intimacy, rather than sexual experience, is the basic goal.

As they told it, these young people, who come from fairly representative middle-class business and professional families, begin their heterosexual experience in groups. Boys and girls hang out together. They eat lunch together in school. They study together, drop off at the same pizza joint on the way home. They keep in touch by phone even when they're apart—as younger girls do—discussing everything from homework to friends and enemies, teachers' behavior and misbehavior, weekend plans, their parents' latest awful unjust act, and family fights.

They go to games and movies. They plan parties at each other's houses where they listen to music, eat, drink Cokes, kid, wrestle a bit. Afterward, instead of pairing off, girls go home together and boys travel with each other.

This pattern may go on for years. Some teen-agers develop platonic friendships, too. Sublimated sexual attraction may be an element, but common intellectual, athletic, aesthetic, and spiritual interests are the cement that holds them together. Platonic friendship sometimes blossoms into love. More typically, the brother-sister relationship has its day. When they are ready, girls and boys mature to true love relationships. While these start as friendships, sexual attraction is always present. After a period of increasing intimacy and growing commitment, the friends become lovers.

None of our study group was engaged in sex for the sake of sex. The single boy and girl who had casual sex were using it to avoid more troubling problems—as is generally the case. Sex problems are almost always symptomatic of basic anxiety about growing up. Children with sex problems usually have few, if any, friends, real difficulty getting along with peers and grownups in authority, and such pervasive insecurity about who they are and what they're worth that they can't "get it together"—as they put it—to do their work, shoulder their responsibilities, and grow up.

They are exactly the children who frighten parents the most. The usual parental reaction is shock, followed by hysterical lectures, cruel and shaming criticism, and heavy restriction—all of which make matters very much worse.

The child's behavior begs for solicitude, support, affection, understanding. When parents withdraw support, the child sees their hostile anger as further proof of her own incompetence and worthlessness. When parents are harshly critical it increases the child's already intense anxiety. The child tends to withdraw. The parent is precluded from gaining her confidence and offering the help and support that is needed.

Parents, like the Smiths and the Joneses, sometimes react almost as inappropriately and unreasonably to their perfectly normal, decent, healthy children. They respond to myths about teen-agers picked up from the media, instead of to their flesh-and-blood children and the actual facts. The mistrust between parent and child that results stimulates exactly the behavior that parents are hoping to prevent.

Parents' fears about teen-age children's sexuality have deep and complex roots. They come from anxiety instilled in the parents' own childhood. They reflect parents' worries about their repressed desires. Fathers' concerns may stem from guilty memories of uncaring episodes with innocent and long-forgotten girls.

If you think a bit about what's behind your reactions, it may keep you from being unreasonable and self-defeating with your daughter.

Sex does not change the way adolescents treat themselves or each other. Kind children stay kind. Decent, responsible, thoughtful children remain that way. Nevertheless, social influences today may put tremendous pressure on adolescents, as on older people, to be "free" and "articulate" sexually. Freedom—particularly among peer-directed teen-agers —may, paradoxically, be read as compulsion. Thus even the steadiest and strongest sometimes have trouble navigating. They need parental direction and control. Misplaced anxiety, suspicious distrust, heavy restrictions, alienate and estrange, at the very time daughters need your support and guidance most.

To go back to the lakeside cottage, Jan's and Ellen's parents lectured, shouted, called names, piled on rules and prohibitions. The children never got a chance to tell where they had been, or what they were doing—all innocent.

The parents closed the door. The girls, as adolescents practicing for independence will do, found a way out of their parents' confines.

Three days later the police knocked on the cottage door at 4 A.M. The girls, whom their parents had seen in bed at ten, had been arrested for breaking and entering. They'd snuck out of their bedroom window when their parents were asleep; met their new friends on Main Street; spent several hours around a bonfire on the beach; gone to an older boy's apartment for food.

Then, looking for *milk*, they'd helped themselves from the nearest deli—which was unlocked. They left a signed note explaining that they'd come back to pay in the morning. This didn't satisfy the policemen who found them as they were leaving.

It would be nice to report that Ellen's and Jan's parents saw the light at this point. Unfortunately they supported the police. Months later, Ellen, once a happy, successful, and mature teen-ager, became a truant. When her parents consulted a psychiatrist, they began to perceive how they had contributed to her problems.

Parents who have gotten along well with their children usually continue to keep their confidence and respect through adolescence—as long as they (the parents) keep their heads. However, adolescents feel much less self-conscious about their own burgeoning sexuality, and more able to talk about it, if parents have been able to show affection to each other easily and to answer questions and talk about

1 6 7

body functions and sex, informally and spontaneously, right
along.

The last thing you want are regular Thursday evening
fireside chats about love, or clinical discussions about sex
and reproduction. Your daughter can get that from books.
It is important to make sure, somewhere in early adolescence, that she knows everything she needs to and wants to
about the simple mechanics of sexual intercourse and reproduction. You want to make sure she is prepared to protect
herself. But, almost more important, you want to convey
your feelings about sexual involvement. You want to give
her a point of view and create a climate in which she can
think and talk about what's important to her.

Your discussions will probably start off quite casually. If
you are alert, you will pick up clues that tell you she has a
question, wants advice, or simply wants to hear how you
feel.

A remark like "Rhoda says lots of sophomores are sleeping with their boy friends" may be a signal that your daughter wants to know whether you think it's okay for *her* to
sleep with her boy friend. The temptation is to spout your
own views at this point. It's better not to. If, instead, you
ask her what she thinks about it, you'll find out what's *really*
on her mind, rather than what you *think* is. You may, in
fact, encourage her to ask what she wants to know directly.

She may tell you she thinks it's dumb (a fairly usual response at fourteen). She may say she thinks it's okay if you
really like the person a lot. She may confess a lot of concerns: Will she get so dependent on her boy friend that she
won't be able to study? What will the boy think? What if
she says no? What will teachers think if they find out? Will
she risk getting pregnant?

Biding your time, getting her opinion before giving

yours, will help you know how to respond, and give you a better opportunity to present your own point of view.

Speak honestly and frankly. *Do not be afraid to disagree.* If your daughter loves and respects you, your views will stick with her and give her something to think about, even if she can't *accept* them. *It's when parents insist that their way is the only way, and all other ways are not only wrong but evil, that teen-agers tune out.*

If you're super-tolerant when you obviously don't share her views, you'll lose her respect and confuse her. She won't be able to trust in your advice and guidance.

If you think premarital sex is wrong or ill-advised, say so. Then tell her, as clearly as you can, why.

If you don't know what's right, say so. There's nothing wrong with being confused. Actually, it's comforting to a teen-ager who is pulled in several directions a great deal of the time. It encourages her to try to figure things out with you.

You may be opposed to all necking and petting until marriage. Your daughter will think you're quaint and touching. She may gradually bring you around, in fact, if you're willing to listen.

You may believe that intercourse is only meaningful when a deep emotional bond exists between the partners. Some daughters may think you're for the Dinosaur Hall, but they'll pay attention.

If you say you think sexual intimacy should be reserved for people who know each other very well, love each other very much, and care a lot for each other, she'll probably smile and nod in agreement.

Whatever your point of view, try ending your statement with "That's how *I* feel. BUT . . ."

Then go on to make it clear that part of growing up is setting your own standards and goals.

169

In outline, you might put it something like this—to suit *your* child and yourselves.

"It's your life. You are learning to judge people as you go along—girls as well as boys. There's no hurry about having sex first. It's not like being first with a new hairdo or style. It involves you in a very personal way. You may be under lots of pressure from "everyone else" at times. You may think your best friends will drop you if you don't join the crowd and have intercourse. Remember your best friends may (1) need support for something they're not sure they're happy about themselves, or (2) be exaggerating their own expertise.

"Boys may push you and make you feel you're old-fashioned or uptight. Maybe they're not the boys for you if they don't respect your feelings. On the other hand, maybe they are trying to prove themselves, or establish their status with their gang. That doesn't matter really if you feel you are close enough friends to be close sexually. If you don't, *you're the boss.* You have never had to behave to please other people. You've always had friends and success being true to yourself. Don't change.

"We realize everyone wants to be 'in.' We know it's hard to be different, but you can be pretty sure that there are plenty of attractive girls and boys who feel pushed to go further than they want to. The easiest thing in the world is just to say, 'No. I'm scared. I don't feel like it. I like you, but I'm not ready.'

"You may just find your friend is as relieved as you are. Boys are under pressure, too, these days to be sexual achievers before they want to be.

"You have never let someone else decide what you should believe or think. Why should you let someone else decide what you should do with your own body? When you do, you give up your independence. You accept that person's definition of who you should be. You forfeit your right to decide who you are for yourself."

With talk like this you convey affection, trust, and caring. Whether your child agrees with what you say or not, you will make her feel loved and respected and worth-while. Your expectations will make her better able to handle the pressures from her peers and come back to you again for re-assurance and guidance when she needs to.

You cannot always be that helpful. Certain situations push otherwise sensible and steady girls into being sexually active against their best judgment and will. When girls mature early and look much older than their years they are sometimes treated as if they *were* older. They have sexual experience before they are ready because they are simply too inexperienced, too vulnerable, to know how to say no.

Girls who look younger have much the same problem. They *try* to 'act' older than they feel, hoping to gain peer approval and be more popular with their age mates.

Sometimes in these situations girls cope with the problem by avoiding it completely. They find soulmates and turn their backs on their peers, dedicating themselves to intel-lectual pursuits, poetry, drama, philosophy. Five years later, happily heterosexual, with congenial lovers or mates, they may look back and laugh.

Some become, almost literally, greasy grinds. They neg-lect their hair, skin, and diet. They reject their physical selves and drudge away at their work with hardly a sidewise glance at their contemporaries. Relatively healthy girls in reasonably happy families use these defenses when they need them and drop them when they're ready for boys. Un-less the child is doing badly in the academic work that has become the focus of her concentration, and unless she is ob-

171

viously unhappy and withdrawn, even with the family, there is no reason for concern. Interference, efforts to "socialize" a child like this, only create anxiety and conflict. You don't want to make her feel strange. She already does.

In these situations parents' efforts can make things worse. Parents' anxiety feeds the child's insecurity, and makes her more aware of her maladaptive method of coping and more concerned about it.

Don't pry. Don't ask questions. Try to conceal worries even if you have them. Wait.

If you're asked for help—and only then—point out that the problem is a common one but neither serious nor permanent. It will be gone tomorrow, when she catches up with her body or her body catches up with her head. Reassurance won't dissolve the pain of the moment. There is nothing more awful to a sociable child than growing up feeling different. She doesn't want parents' love and understanding. She wants to be one of the crowd. Nevertheless, in a pinch, parents' love and belief is better than nothing.

Rules and regulations won't help the child who is solving her problems by going sex-wild, but they may help protect her. In fact restrictions, even when resented, are a crutch many adolescents need when they are still unsure about their judgment and their ability to resist the rule of their peers.

Progressive, trusting parents feel it is somehow belittling to give teen-age children rules. "After all," as we have heard them say again and again, "they know what we stand for. They share our views."

This may all be so. But it is also important to realize that adolescents, with the best will in the world, have not always developed the moral muscle to stand up in a party and say, "This is too much. I'm going home," or tell a boy who wants to go driving after the movie, "I think I know what you're up to and I don't want it."

Your rules give them noes until they can say their own. Your children may indeed argue and sulk and even say mean things to you. Stand firm. Until very late in their high school careers most adolescents need restrictions. Find out whether adults will be present at parties. Check with the host parents. Set reasonable but firm curfews. Make sure your daughter understands that she must call you if she changes her plans in the course of the evening, and cannot be home as agreed.

Many parents of adolescents wonder whether they should dispense contraceptive advice. The question is a delicate one. You don't want your child to feel that you are pushing sex. Still, it is realistic to anticipate that she may need protection if the teen-age community she is in condones premarital sex.

If you know your child may need contraceptive advice, talk about it. You cannot assume that a child knows about birth control and is practicing it just because she is practicing sex. If this were so we would not be experiencing a continuing rise in childbirth among teen-agers in the face of a declining national birth rate.

Not long ago a seventeen-year-old girl, Judy, asked if she could have her boy friend for the weekend. When her mother told her to get the guest room ready Judy announced that they were sleeping together.

Her mother was neither surprised nor disapproving. She liked the boy. As she told us, "Judy has always had good judgment in friends." She was glad to have an appropriate opportunity to find out whether Judy was properly protected. She found that the boy was practicing *coitus interruptus*—a precarious form of contraception, especially for a teen-ager. Judy agreed it would be safer to get a doctor's advice. Her mother recommended a specialist in adolescent medicine, saying, "It's about time you gave up your pediatrician." Judy was happy to go—*if* her mother would make the appointment.

Adolescents in some respects are still children, still uncomfortable with the grown-up aspects of their roles. The fact that many doctors embarrass them when they do ask for contraceptive help gets around, and makes it harder for them to get medical advice. It's easier and safer to help them along. It's better to risk offending a girl by suggesting contraception than it is to risk an accident. Offer advice. Even if it is rudely rejected with "I know all about it. It's none of your business."

If that happens, you need only say, "I'm interested in your safety. I don't mean to intrude at all. As long as you're not taking chances, that's all I need to know."

This may be a good place to repeat the truism. You can't be perfect. Children can't be perfect. Sometimes, in spite of your devoted efforts, problems develop, persist, and get worse. Parent-child relations can be rough. Advice doesn't always work. Some children refuse to listen and seem destined to have to learn from their own mistakes and suffering. Accidents will happen. It sounds smug to advise patience and understanding help when they do. It seems insensitive to tell you to treat an unwanted pregnancy, a shocking sexual encounter, or a rape as if it were a playground spill: "Pick her up; hug and comfort." Yet that's the best advice we can give. The love and concern a parent shows in what, to a girl, is a moment of deep shame and rejection, can be a turning point in her development. There will be time enough to talk when the crisis is over. The knowledge that you cared for her and loved her when she felt least worthy will linger and perhaps persuade her to care for herself and take her future seriously.

174

As we pointed out in Chapter Seven, girls seem to have more anxiety-provoking questions and problems than boys do in adolescence. Can they be feminine and loving, with all the softness and acceptance that implies to them, and still pursue their adventurous goals and intense drive for achievement and self-expression? Can they belong to a man and still control their lives? Can they be mothers? Do they want to be? If not, why not? If they choose a new and different way to be women, will they sacrifice happiness, friendship, respect, protection?

The questions are obviously complicated by the times. Men's and women's roles are changing so fast that it's hard for the individual to define what's right for herself. Sometimes it's easier to accept a rather stereotyped new image of womanhood than to work out the one that suits.

Parents don't know the answers. You may wish you had the supreme confidence in your supreme judgment that your parents did. You may sometimes wish you could abdicate responsibility. But you can't. If you understand and sympathize with your daughter's problems and communicate, by example and word, comfortable feelings about yourselves as men and women, and about her, she will keep coming to you for comfort, support, and guidance until she resolves her problems, or outgrows them.

If you don't know how to talk easily to teen-agers, confess it. And don't feel *too* inadequate. What children need most, right through childhood, whether the issue is sex, how to fight, or how to make up with a friend, is the knowledge that their parents like them, care for them, and trust them. This helps them build their self-confidence. Self-confidence is the cornerstone of maturity.

SUGGESTED READING LIST

For Young Children (*Ages 4–9*)

Andry, Andrew C., and Schepp, Steven. *How Babies Are Made.* New York: Time-Life Books, 1968.

De Schweinitz, Karl. *Growing Up: How We Become Alive, Are Born and Grow.* New York: Collier, 1974 (paperback).

Gruenberg, Sidonie Matsner. *The Wonderful Story of How You Were Born.* Garden City, N.Y.: Doubleday & Company, 1970; Doubleday Zephyr Book paperback.

Nilsson, Lennart. *How I Was Born.* New York: Delacorte Press, 1975.

For Pre- and Early Teens (*Ages 10–14*)

Gordon, Sol, Ph.D. *Facts About Sex for Today's Youth.* New York: John Day, 1973 (paperback).

Pomeroy, Wardell B., Ph.D. *Girls and Sex.* New York: Dell, 1973 (paperback).

For Later Teens (*Ages 15–18*)

Liebeman, E. James, M.D., and Peck, Ellen. *Sex and Birth Control: A Guide for the Young.* New York: Schocken Books, 1975 (paperback).

Mazur, Ronald. *Commonsense Sex.* Boston, Mass.: Beacon Press, 1973 (paperback).

Preston, Harry, with Margolin, Jeanette, M.D. *Everything a Teenager Wants to Know About Sex . . . and Should.* New York: Books for Better Living, 1973 (paperback).

Southard, Helen. *Sex Before Twenty: New Answers for Youth.* New York: E. P. Dutton, 1971 (paperback).

For Adults (Age 18 and Over)

Boston Women's Health Book Collective. *Our Bodies, Ourselves.* rev. ed. New York: Simon & Schuster, 1976 (paperback). Also from N.E. Free Press, 791 Fremont St., Boston, Mass. 02118.

Brenton, Myron. *Sex Talk.* New York: Fawcett, 1973.

Calderone, Mary, M.D. *Sexuality and Human Values.* New York: Association Press, 1975.

McCary, James Leslie, Ph.D. *Sexual Myths and Fallacies.* New York: Schocken Books, 1973 (paperback).

This list has been prepared with the cooperation of SIECUS (Sex Information and Education Council of the U.S., 137–155 North Franklin, Hempstead, L.I., N.Y., 11550). Complete reading lists with descriptive comments are available from SIECUS.

NOTES

[1] Stella Chess, M.D., Alexander Thomas, M.D., and Martha Cameron, "Sexual Attitudes and Behavior Patterns in a Middle Class Adolescent Population," *American Journal of Orthopsychiatry,* Vol. 46, No. 4 (October 1976), pp. 689–701.

CHAPTER TEN

Letting Go

Recently we were listening to a college professor talk about her daughter: "She was telling me about her dissertation. Suddenly I realized, my child knows more about this work than I can ever hope to. She's my peer. It was very exciting."

We don't all have these illuminating flashes. But sometime after children leave home for college or another route to independence the parent-child relationship changes.

Children face new challenges at every age. They complete their tasks and move on to more demanding ones. As they mature, they become more responsible. Parents ideally become less responsible. They adapt their role to the child's needs at each successive stage of development. Finally, if all goes well, they are "phased out" completely. Moral, emotional, and financial responsibility for the child comes to an end.

Legal responsibility ends when children reach eighteen or

finish high school. But breaking the parent-child bond of childhood is not that quick and easy. For years longer, middle-class parents pay out, supervise, advise and consent. Financial responsibility may continue well into a child's adult life, depending on the career she chooses and the time it takes to prepare for it. Emotional dependence is something else. It may go on long after a child is off the family payroll. The most important task of children in the post–high school years is to learn to function independently without being bound by parents' wishes or inhibited by their disapproval. Paradoxically, they need parents' help to make the getaway successfully. For parents, the trick is to watch the children's take-off attempts, standing by unobtrusively for back up, and pay the way, without exacting such high interest and strict accounting that the children never get a chance to fly alone.

If you and your child succeed in your respective tasks the parent-child relationship will gradually evolve. You will never stop being THE parent. Your child will remain forever, in your eyes and her own, YOUR child, with all the eternal implications of the bond. But you will become, as well, friends and equals—in the sense our professor friend describes—with the precious difference that your particular history together gives the relationship.

As children approach the end of high school, they anticipate almost physically the prospect of breaking loose at last. They express it in many different ways.

In some communities, high school commencement is followed by an almost ritualistic declaration of independence. In marathon-like compulsion the graduates dance, drink, smoke, drive, socialize, and sexualize till dawn. There is only one rule: You can't go home and go to bed.

The morning after is often a sobering experience. The graduates may imagine that they are now rid of all those nasty old people telling them what to do. They wake up to discover—wherever they are—that the DICTATORS still exist, as well as their PARENTS. They realize, sooner or later, that freedom takes more than declaring one's independence.

Learning to be free—doing what you want to do, going where you want to go, without feeling compelled by parents or others to take the course you're on—is a long and complex undertaking.

The person who doesn't ever feel constrained, anxious, or ambivalent about other people's (particularly parents') opinion, whatever her age, is unreal. The free person, however, can stay on the path she's chosen, *in spite of powerful opposition,* or reconsider calmly and switch to a more congenial one if the switch seems warranted.

In the long-term interests of one's independent way, one learns to make compromises and concessions and to accept discipline, often quite rigid rules, restrictions, and domination.

Learning to be free, to lead an independent life, requires knowing yourself, knowing what you want, making the choices necessary to advance your goals. It takes will, spirit, and courage to judge the opposition objectively and not be thrown off or sidetracked just to avoid examining it. It takes a knack for knowing when and how to goof off for rest and relaxation or experimental purposes, without getting permanently diverted or giving up.

Learning to be free requires learning that freedom is *relative.* Who is independent? No one ever is, completely and consistently. And that is a most important thing for parents to realize and children to learn in these years. Learning to be independent takes time. Not many young people can handle freedom and use it to find their independent ways without a fairly lengthy period of trial and error.

If you are lucky—and chance can be crucial in this period

—your daughter will make the transition from school to college, travel, or work so smoothly that scarcely a ripple will mark her passage.

Some people just naturally ease into things—new jobs, new houses, new marriages: what have you. It's their nature to make friends easily. It's easy for them to decide what they want to do and sit down and do it.

Some children have strong likes and dislikes, or a well-defined talent or interest they have wanted to concentrate on, undistracted, since early or middle childhood. They can't wait for the chance to get on with it.

But many more children need time after high school to look around and experiment beside advisers they trust, with experienced models to follow. Finally, with the luck of a parachuting pilot landing in a barrel of goose down, they will come through, more or less independent adults.

What can parents expect in the interim? How can you help?

The Morning-after Syndrome

Yesterday's jubilant high school graduate wakes up in the college of her choice, free at last. Slowly, but with increasing intensity, it begins to dawn upon her that *college* was *not her* choice. She realizes she is there *without her will.* She is suddenly aware of the remorseless system that has put her on the college track and led her to spend her high school years compiling a college record (sports, leadership, social position, grades, community good works, job experience).

Her freshman courses in huge lecture halls, brought to her, amplified, by faceless voices, sound like yet another repeat of the courses she feels she has been taking over and over since fourth grade. History begins with one day on prehistory and ends at World War II. Her dreams are full of course credits, credit ratios, major requirements, graduation requirements. Now, she says, she wants to get off the treadmill. She wants to stop doing what everyone has always told her to do and start practicing independence.

Whether her feelings accurately reflect reality is beside the point. They are her feelings. And, in point of fact, in a certain segment of our society children are led by parents and schools to do everything in their power to get to the college of their choice: i.e., the most difficult possible one. Some children have their schools' and their parents' informed and altruistic guidance and undoubtedly know what they're doing. Others go fairly blindly, fueled by a kind of dreamy fantasy that, once they're there, college, like Pandora's box, will offer limitless goodies.

No matter how they got to college, a certain number are going to suffer the morning-after syndrome: an overwhelming feeling that it was not their informed choice, and an almost compulsive need to remedy the situation.

Some will insist that they must leave posthaste. Some will shilly-shally, getting nowhere. Some will flunk out, semiconsciously. Some will drop out.

Parents, however much they want to, often have a hard time helping. Some children are ashamed to ask for help. They are stuck with the symbolic meaning of leaving home. They feel they have to "hack it," as they say. They feel obliged to make up their own minds and handle everything alone. They think they must be victims of arrested development if they can't.

The fantasy that everything will be all right once they get out of your clutches nourishes many children through the high school years. They are constitutionally incapable of entertaining the idea that you could have anything of value to say. They are also determined to believe that you are just waiting for a chance to start giving orders again.

183

The fact that you have had a pleasant, positive, give-and-take relationship with a daughter doesn't necessarily make a difference. The need to assert independence outweighs this. In fact, the happier and more comfortable a daughter's relationship with parents has been, the more urgent the need to terminate it may seem right now.

Before children can learn how to live with parents and still live apart from them, they often need to go far away, emotionally speaking. Before they can take help and guidance from you, no matter how much they may need and even secretly want it, you have to show them they can trust you all over again. You have to coax them into testing what the new relationship can be.

They have to discover the difference between advice and orders. They have to be able to recognize the difference between "Turn off the TV until you get your homework done" and "This is my *advice*. It's not necessarily infallible or even the best. Ask other people. Think about it." They have to learn how to ask questions and use advice to help them make decisions of their own. They have to learn to use the voice of experience for guidance instead of letting it take over.

They learn sooner if you can outline possibilities, offer alternatives, and ask questions *instead of:*

1. FRIGHTENING AND THREATENING: "If you don't go to college you're on your own. Remember—that's final."

2. ACCUSING: "You don't appreciate. You're spoiled. . . ."

3. SOUNDING HYSTERICAL: "You'll never get anywhere if . . ."

Try, as far as you are able, to keep a dialogue with your daughter going through what we might call the "programmed" years. If it is regularly stated and clearly understood in your household that no one's program after high school is preordained, it will be easier for your children to withstand the pressures of the community, whatever they may be. You have been helping your daughter to anticipate her future from the day she drew a picture and you said, half in fun, "Going to be an artist when you grow up?"

During the high school years the discussion can become more serious, without becoming pushy or threatening. You can confide some of your abandoned adolescent goals and talk about why you gave them up. Evaluate the consequences together. If you were pushed by necessity or a force stronger than yours to a career you didn't choose, it will be instructive to her to talk about how it turned out. What are your regrets, if any, today? What would your advice be to someone in that position today? Did you gain unanticipated benefits from the forced choice?

This kind of discussion dissolves the distance between you, makes you more accessible, takes you out of the infallible, far-off authority role parents seem to have to younger children. Your daughter may gain a new view of life from you.

Talk that begins casually, stimulated by such apparently trivial stuff as a news item about a middle-aged family taking off in a sailboat for the kind of life they've dreamed of but never dared to lead, encourages children to confess their own dreams and hopes. Hearing how they sound to you encourages serious thinking about the future. Ask friendly, serious questions. Don't make fun or cut off with devastating criticism.

Try to make your children feel that thinking about and planning their lives and talking about different possibilities for careers and study and ways of life is exciting, rather than threatening, ominous, super-important, crucial. Be sure they realize that their lives are theirs to plan and live.

Make it clear that, whatever you may have provided for them or prepared them for, nothing is preordained; nothing should be dictated by your wishes or community pressures. Encourage daughters in the later high school years to start thinking seriously about where they want to go next instead of letting them go lock-step to college. It may avoid second thoughts, and wasted time and money.

Americans *send* their children to college if they possibly can, and sometimes even when they can't, or shouldn't. A few generations ago girls took piano lessons, just as they wore Mary Janes to parties. Whether a child could hear one note from another, or had any interest in music *or* the piano, was immaterial. In fact, most children read music by learning to associate notes on the score with black or white keys on the piano. The music was irrelevant. Children bold enough to complain were told to endure and promised that they would be glad later. Few were glad, and they probably were not the complainers.

Middle- and upper-class parents send their children to college because they always have. Other families send theirs because they never had a chance themselves. Parents don't stop often enough to consider whether a child will benefit from college or whether it might indeed be counterproductive.

It took the bold young people who some years back protested the irrelevancy of college to their interests and goals to wake us up to the possibility of viable alternatives to four more academic years.

The only people who clearly should go to college are those who truly want to after they have had a chance to see and hear for themselves from older friends, teachers, trusted relatives, and personal exposure what goes on there.

These include, generally:

1. Girls who have been serious students and have already decided on their field of interest.

2. Solid students who look forward to a stimulating four years in an environment that will allow them time to grow up and find out what they want to do with their grown-up lives.

3. Girls who know they want to be doctors, lawyers, architects, scholars, and teachers, or follow some other career for which a baccalaureate is the basic prerequisite. Not only do they need college. The fact that they are set about where they are going suggests that they will probably gain from their college experience.

Many children should never go to college, and many more should go later, if ever, when they have a better idea of what they're going for.

Young people who want to be artists, craftspeople, film makers, photographers, composers, performers, mechanics, artisans, carpenters, plumbers, or electricians don't need college. They do need special training. They may feel they have no time for college, though they may come back to it. They may claim they know enough to learn whatever else they want to on their own.

It is much too late at this age to *tell* them how to lead their lives. It is time now for them to take control of themselves and assume responsibility for the outcome.

If you've been talking to each other right along, you can judge the merits of your daughter's decision and whether she has a decent chance of benefiting from her choice. If you haven't been talking, here's a place to start.

Some parents treat a child who wants to be an artist or craftsperson, or to make a living with her hands, as if she were playing at life, wasting time. They refuse to take such plans seriously. If you hear your daughter out you may be surprised to learn how deeply she's thought about what she wants to do. You will also be able to review the plans to see how practical they are. If you respect her wishes you will make her take herself more seriously and perhaps make a more committed effort to succeed in her plans.

You might want to check whether the art school she has picked is really qualified to give her the kind of training she wants. You might suggest the possibility of an art school that has a tie-in with a liberal arts college. The Bachelor of Fine Arts degree that she would earn would expand her options on graduation. She could practice art as she now intends, or go on for an advanced degree that would qualify her to teach, or do museum or gallery work to help support herself while she continues to practice art.

She may want to take a year off to relax, sort out feelings about her past, present, and future, and get some perspective. If you've been working and saving ever since she was born so she could *go* to college, her indifference to it may strike you as irresponsible, even selfish. If you hear your daughter out before reacting, you may react differently. Concern about spending parents' money when they don't feel ready to make the most of college is often a major factor in young people's reluctance to go.

When children have no plans they tend to react against what they see as "your" plans for them rather than consider alternatives. If you respect their right to be confused or fed up at the start, they begin to think more constructively and often welcome your guidance.

Try to build on the parts of their lives they feel good about. If a girl likes working with children, ask her if she would like to work in a children's hospital, a clinic, a school for troubled or handicapped children, a day-care center. If your daughter likes clothes, help her find out about work in the fashion industry—advertising, merchandising, wholesale manufacturing, and sales.

She may be starved for a chance to learn something just for fun, not for her college record—music, for instance. Encourage her spontaneous enthusiasms.

You don't have to accept the sabbatical as a foregone conclusion until you've talked about it at length and repeatedly. There are alternatives to the high-pressured boarding college that might seem more inviting.

She could start in a community college and live at home; take courses (with credit) at a college or university within commuting distance and work part-time; try college with the understanding that she might drop out after a semester or a year. She might consider a totally different kind of college from the ones her school assumed she would aim for.

If you have a strong hunch (as distinct from personal desire) that your daughter will finally want to get a college degree, you might ask her to consider the possibility of gaining admission to college now, when taking exams will be easier, just in case she wants to enter later.

Planning is important, too, to keep the year off from being a "nothing" year: a year so aimless, unchallenging, and unproductive that she will feel less organized and more confused about her goals at the end than she was at the beginning.

Planning should be realistic. Young people want a hiatus from study in order to catch their breath. They want a chance to step aside from the influence of the teachers, grandparents, and parents whom they feel they have been working for all their lives. They aren't always perfectly certain that they won't eventually want to follow your program for them. But they are sure they want time to think about themselves, consider for themselves, and decide for themselves.

To do this, they need to *be* apart from you, particularly financially. They can't really stand on their own at your expense. Whether you can afford to support the sabbatical year or not is irrelevant.

An angry boy once complained to us that his parents didn't recognize his need for independence because they wouldn't pay the rent for his apartment. You don't learn independence on an allowance from home.

If a girl has to figure out how to support herself, she's likely to think more seriously about what she wants to gain from her time out. A little experience trying to get the money to live on at the low hourly rates most inexperienced high school graduates can command sometimes stimulates second thoughts. Studying music sounds nice if the bills are all paid by magic (parents). It may seem less interesting when she has to work between guitar or sitar lessons or composition classes to support herself.

Travel sounds dreamy: no time limits, no definite itinerary. A seventeen-year-old imagines starting out with the bank accounts saved up from Christmas, birthday, and graduation presents since birth, and just going. Knowing there is $1,000, period, changes the picture. She knows she can't cable home. She knows she may not, and probably won't, find work in Turkey. *So* . . . she has to think where she's going, and why, and plan her trip so that she can stop at regular intervals where there may be a chance to earn money.

Independence introduces reality. Reality often provides the focus many young people need to help them begin to think about their goals and how to reach them.

Dropping Out

Lots of perfectly normal freshmen and sophomores reach a point where they feel they have to drop out. They are not usually secretive about their intentions, but generally give fair warning. The fair warning is a signal for talk.

First, try to assess the situation. Is it a temporary crisis? Is it a case of freshman slump; goof-off; delayed adjustment to college schedules, college work, and independence? If it is one of the latter, advice from the college guidance department, reassurance from you that failure need not be final, and perhaps some quite specific coaching on how to schedule time, budget time, and preplan long assignments will help.

If it's a case of being bored, feeling numb and exhausted, really wanting to get a change, dropping out is probably a good idea.

If your child is determined to leave, she will probably want to pack up and get out today. Persuade her, if you can, to keep her options open. Coax the freshman to finish her term and collect her credits in case of return. Dissuade the senior from leaving before final examinations. Ask her to get extensions on her papers if she's hopelessly behind. Investigate leaves of absence, as an alternative to simply quitting.

Dropouts, like stay-outs, need plans to work on. Here, too, ground rules should include the requirement to be self-supporting while on furlough. Plans don't need to be drawn up and presented in triplicate at the first parent-child discussion. Nor should your child feel compelled to gain your unqualified approval, at first or even fifth meeting. The decision about what to do should finally be the dropout's. If it is, she's likely to feel more responsible about working out

191

her own way to independence. Whether you approve or not, make it clear that you are willing to help whenever you can, with advice, ideas, experience and/or referrals to other advisers or potential employers.

"It's up to you" can mean two things to a college freshman: "You're old enough to decide and capable enough to decide for yourself. Go to it," or "I wash my hands of you. You made your bed. Lie in it!"

Even if you feel like washing your hands of her, you won't feel that way for long. Try to take the more supportive attitude *without* taking over support. Try to convey respect while making clear that you expect positive moves toward independence in the dropout period.

Here are some tips that help us when we are trying to help young people sort themselves out. Maybe they'll prove useful.

· Nothing has to be decided today or tomorrow. Discussions don't have to have a beginning, a middle, and an end. Remembering this helps remind you not to bear down too hard or push a discussion beyond where a child feels comfortable with it. You get further sometimes when you stop shorter.

· Don't push discussions when they get stuck. If a question seems to hit a tender spot and there's no adequate answer, or none at all, let it drop, *even though* you feel "we really ought to clear this up."

If there is no answer the issue is probably an important one. Raising it will stimulate the child's thinking. If she can, she'll come back to it on her own, later.

· Try to be honest about your own feelings and hopes for your child. Try to see and hear what she is talking about from *her* perspective. Remember where she is and where

192

you are. It's better to tell her your feelings, fears, and goals and what's behind them than to pretend you are acting solely in her interest, as the impartial voice of experience.

· Give opinions; don't make pronouncements. Respect her reactions to your ideas. Make them the basis for discussion. Your commands may still have the ring of authority, but your opinions should not be sacred. They should stimulate discussion rather than stifle it. If she doesn't agree, talk— don't intimidate by putting her ideas down.

· Ask yourself now and then, "Am I ready to let go?" Review your feelings and reactions and the positions you've taken in discussions with your daughter. Are you really helping her learn to think for herself and make independent choices? Or are you making her too cautious about taking off on her own course, by throwing up too many obstacles?

Troubled or Ill?

This is probably an appropriate place to talk about mental illness and how to distinguish the normal, normally troubled young person from one who is seriously ill.

The decisions that go with growing up and leaving home are hard ones. They require a lot of close self-examination. The more vulnerable adolescents can't always take the stress.

A great deal has been written about the identity crisis and the alienation that often attends it. Parents have wisely taken notice. It is, however, important to distinguish between the normal fears, anxiety, rebelliousness, and moodiness of adolescence and symptoms of severe illness.

Young people who are headed for serious trouble generally give off warning signals. Their behavior changes markedly. The friendly may become unreasonably irritable, or

193

silent and withdrawn. Academic performance may change abruptly. Depression may cause serious inability to concentrate, to remember, or just to get going at all. A deeply depressed young person will gather books and materials for a project, then simply move around them, apparently unable to decide what to do first, or organize the simplest task. Normal doubts and indecision about what to do or where to go become overpowering. Uncharacteristic, tactless, graceless, sneering behavior—even in public—is a sign of trouble. Overeating or loss of appetite may be symptoms. So are insomnia, abnormal need for sleep, and unwillingness to get up.

Friends and teachers usually recognize something is wrong and try to guide disturbed young people to a guidance teacher or doctor. If the child is at home, parents would have no trouble recognizing the signs of incipient illness. If you are concerned about your child it is better to be too protective than too casual. It is difficult for parents to be objective in such circumstances. They also lack experience to distinguish between severe illness and some of the more dramatic manifestations of temporary but normal adolescent misery. If you have doubts, consult a doctor at once.

The Prison of Sexual Freedom

Earlier we mentioned a rather common problem of late adolescence: how to say no to sex.

Boys complain about it as much as girls do. However, since boys are still, traditionally, in the role of the aggressor in sexual matters they can choose when to aggress. They have only their male peers and themselves to account to if they decline to aggress at all. Girls, in the more passive role, must take an active stand to say no. In the present climate of sexual freedom that is sometimes hard.

We bring children up to be kind, tender, and considerate of others' feelings. We have tried to make them feel that sex is natural and normal—nothing to fear or feel guilty about. But in our efforts to prevent sexual inhibition, we sometimes come on sounding as if sexual feelings were some kind of universal tic that comes and goes and doesn't mean a thing. We may fail to convey how very personal, private, and *individual* sexual responsiveness is.

As a result, while there is more sexual activity than there used to be, there is not much more understanding of how to cope with sexual feelings. Most girls are still brought up to be attractive and pleasing to men even when they are taught to be individuals. They still have more trouble saying no than boys do. Rejecting a boy's friendly advances seems hostile and unfriendly. They find it hard to respect their own feelings and wishes. If they don't want sex, they feel cornered. They worry because they're not interested. If sex is supposed to be natural, normal, and universal, then they must be abnormal.

They feel uncomfortable, if not unfeminine, about saying no. Some say yes and suffer. Some say no and suffer. Some withdraw from their peers. In this era of sexual freedom, inability to deal with sex seems as common as it ever was. In fact, we have found it to be a factor in the decision of many young people to retreat to the shelter of religious sects that practice the ascetic life, including abstinence.

"Instant" sex is not normal. One cannot be sexually liberated under compulsion. If you have not said this explicitly in casual talks with your daughter during her adolesence, create an occasion now.

Try to rehumanize sex so that your daughter will feel free to express herself sexually rather than feel compelled to be instantly available, willing or not.

Guidebooks for parents can make you feel that you will have full control of your children if you read the directions and follow them carefully enough. Parents and authors have to remind themselves constantly that things just don't turn out that easily, that often.

Guidebooks are just *guide*books, nothing more. Children are unpredictable, changeable, individual—not machines. Instructions are at best *generally* useful. They must be adapted to fit the child, the parents, and the occasion. Sometimes they have to be thrown out the window. With experience, you gradually recognize when to ignore the experts and depend on instinct, intuition, and experience for guides.

So, after a chapter on how to talk to your high school graduate, let's remind ourselves that some children *won't talk*—especially in the years from sixteen to twenty. Valuable as it may be to have a dialogue with your daughter, as she stumbles, shuffles, or leaps into adult independence, there are times when the harder you try, the harder you fail.

Many young teen-agers resist sex talks with their parents. Many older ones resist discussing anything. We remember a very independent five-year-old who used to wait until her mother was out of the house to engage in rather daring baking projects—including lighting a gas oven with a MATCH. She deliberately violated the rules in full knowledge of the consequences because she wanted to see what she could do without anybody's INTERFERENCE.

There may be something of this element in the behavior of a high school junior in our study group. His parents worried about him because he had taken himself out of his prestigious neighborhood high school and moved to a gigantic inner-city school, without consulting them. They thought it was a mistake and might affect his chances of making the college he was trying for. He refused to talk.

When his parents suggested he talk to us, he did so with no hesitancy. The kids in his old school weren't serious, he explained. He was serious. He found the atmosphere and the students in the city school more congenial and stimulating. It was clear that he would get into a college that suited him. He wasn't interested in prestige—he was interested in learning.

When we asked why he couldn't tell all this to his parents, he shrugged his shoulders. "I wanted to do this myself. I knew I was right: it's my life. I've been talking to them for seventeen years."

Some children clam up because they hate defending themselves on parents' terms. Some are still shaky, in spite of their basic conviction and determination about what they are doing. There are times, too, when children simply have to "fly now" and talk later. Whether they soar or flop, parents should let them try.

If you succeed, you will have your reward later, when, like the mother and daughter we started off this chapter with, you face each other with love, admiration, and mutual respect, and recognize you are grownups, independent, but still together.

CHAPTER ELEVEN

After She's Gone Away

Now it's all over. She's out of the house, out of your budget. No more of *her* rings on *your* bathtub. No more of those long nights you lay awake when she didn't come home and didn't call. No more responsibility for the ungrateful, care-free, careless, messy, noisy, argumentative, independent, disaster-prone, difficult . . . Ummm . . . yes . . . ummmm. Loving nostalgia bubbles up. You may miss her already. Probably you miss her friends. Probably you miss the fresh, airy, sassy, enthusiastic, adventurous, *young* air they brought to your house and your lives.

You may be glad to draw that big, deep, free breath at last and talk about what you'll do together, alone at last, with all that expense out of the way. But you may also want her back. It's an off-again, on-again sensation at first. Then it's a kind of constant distraction, like the feeling that alerts you to the fact that something is missing: you've dropped your gloves or left your briefcase behind.

When children graduate from the family, some parents scramble around furiously proving it's great by "making new lives" for themselves. Some mope. Some fight with each other. Some love every minute—even the distraction that reminds them that the package they've carried doesn't *need* to be picked up ever again. Some go back for the package and fuss over it, looking for dents and damage, worrying about what happened to it while it was out of their protective care and supervision.

Retirement isn't easy for everyone. Superannuated parents may have to adjust. When your daughter was two going on three, you dropped her at nursery school, sunny and brisk, your mind already leaping ahead to the day's first appointment. She clung. She may have cried, her mind still with you. Now you may feel a little as she did then. You don't cling or cry, but you sometimes wish her husband, or lover, or work, or vacation would go away and you could have her all to yourself again just as it used to be.

Finally, you adjust to losing her, just as she adjusted to leaving you. Through the long years of child rearing we like to fantasize about what it will be like when children are off for good. We imagine ourselves luxuriating in unfamiliar self-indulgence while we remain thick as thieves with our children, on demand (ours, of course). That's not the way it ever is. We know it even as we spin the fantasy. Fantasy and fable are always a bit bigger and better than life. Nevertheless, the fabled riches of being postgraduate parents to children with lives of their own are real. Many parents discover them. With a bit of foresight and planning, you may, too.

Friends Plus

You can never take back your parenthood. You *can* redefine it. When children grow up and go off, you shed responsibility and become better friends. Think of yourselves as friends plus. Follow the code that guides your friendships: trust, be trustworthy; confide, keep confidence; be indulgent, forgiving, slow to criticize, slow to take offense, quick to praise and comfort, generous and appreciative, congenial, solicitous without prying, helpful without dominating.

Naturally, it's not just like friendship. The plus of parenthood has a way of intruding unpleasantly from time to time.

It's easy to be friends plus when your daughter is thousands of miles away, busy and presumably happy at work and play. It gets progressively harder as distance shrinks.

Letting Go

Suppose your child is *not* quite set yet. She's unhappy in love or just in the doldrums, sick of her job, not sure where to go, or whether to change course. You feel the familiar tug when you see her. Maybe you don't actually put on the chicken soup, but figuratively speaking you do. You cluck and fuss. You want to know all about it. You have the solution on the tip of your tongue—and give it, insistently. You call for progress reports. You advise some more. You begin to nag a bit, maybe, if she seems reluctant to talk. You review her problems with her just as if she were still a teenager. You master-mind her life as if she were your biggest Monopoly holding.

Then you grow cross because "she asks for help and

doesn't follow my advice" or "she might as well be living with me—she takes so much of my time and energy."

There are times when parents have to get involved in grown-up children's lives. Generally speaking, however, if parents curb the familiar impulse to step in and show how anything and everything could be done better, children adjust to being on their own faster, and parents and children end up better and closer friends.

Very deeply involved parents naturally have more trouble disengaging themselves than those who have been letting their children go gradually over the years.

Anticipate the problem before it develops. Then check your reflexes. Make your unconscious reactions conscious: that may help you restrain them. Play cool even when your natural impulse is to barge in, ask questions, and offer help, comfort, advice.

Learn by doing. If you find yourselves acting too much like anxious, protective, *helpful* parents with singular lack of success, remember to try a different tack the next time. When you feel you have to play the heavy parent, treat her like a friend instead. Ask if you can help, instead of telling her what to do.

Keep reminding yourself of *your*self at twenty-five or thirty. Can you remember the state of your mind, career, or finances? Can you recall the problems? Who solved them? You or your parents? Did your parents' concern, unilateral advice, or hovering intrusion make you more or less nervous, anxious, and unsure of yourself? Did it change the course of your life?

If, by remote chance, your parents helped, try to copy them now. If they didn't, which is more likely, perhaps that memory will help keep you from intruding now.

How can you restrain yourself when you feel so needed? Get involved somewhere else. We don't mean needlepoint, community action, or Chinese cooking in the high school's adult education program. We're talking about changing the focus of your relations with your daughter. Whatever your daughter and you, vicariously, are worried about, it shouldn't be the full-time focus of your attention—or even of your daughter's—when you are together. It's easy to make your relationship problem-centered. You start asking innocent questions, just to get news, and you end up approving, disapproving, telling how, telling what to do next: "Where have you been?" "How much did you make?" "Did you get the promotion/raise?" "Where is that nice man you used to bring?" "If you did this, maybe then . . ."

Sometimes when parents are troubled about small children we help them put the problem in perspective by getting them to talk about what they enjoy in the child, what they admire, find amusing, empathize with. We talk about what parts of parenting they like best: reading stories, telling stories, teaching, introducing the child to their own interests, going to museums, cooking or making things together.

You can use this device now. Plan for your visits together. Arrange to spend them doing what interests you both, talking about things you both care about. If your daughter needs your help, let her be the first to announce it. If you're asked for advice, give it. Then move on. You'll feel better when she leaves, and so will she.

You may not untangle yourself completely from your old apron strings, but you won't get your daughter knotted up in them with you. And someday in the future—maybe tomorrow, maybe a year from now—you'll realize that you've let her go. You may start off worrying as usual about Felicity's unhappiness with Joe: "Felicity is upset about Joe. What can she do? What can I do?" Then all of a sudden truth will descend. "Nothing, nothing at all," you'll find yourself saying, and meaning it. "I can't change Felicity. I can't change Joe. That's life. She'll feel better."

You'll send her a record you know she wants or ask her to dinner, with her favorite food or her favorite cousin, and be surprised to note that she doesn't seem so unhappy after all.

Overinvolvement isn't always parents' doing. Grown children can entice you, even embroil you. Why not? What are families for? Why shouldn't you be the first to get the bad news, just as you hope to be the first to hear of minor coups and major triumphs? Parents expect grown-up children to confide in them and ask advice. What they don't always like is having to be all-responsible again, just as children, if they're really grown-up, don't like being made to feel like helpless kids all over again.

You can usually avoid this situation if you remember to remember that your role has changed.

Careers, money, love, marriage, and children are the dominating problems of young adulthood. And these are the very matters that often get parents and their children into deep trouble with each other.

Advise, if you're asked, but don't criticize. Point out the advantages and disadvantages of alternative courses as you see things. Leave the decisions to her. If you have strong differences of opinion and your way turns out to have been the wiser one, avoid "I told you so" at any cost. If you can find some positive value in the experience, point it out, instead of contributing to the prevailing gloom.

Financial Problems

Children usually turn to parents first when they need financial advice or help. Sometimes parents' help works. Sometimes the way they help simply perpetuates a pattern of dependency. Some children rely on parents the way they probably did, long after they should have, in childhood. Parents continue to bail them out, instead of letting them learn to live responsibly with the realities of life.

When this happens, parents and child get locked into a two-way bind. She needs money. You give it, more and more reluctantly, afraid that she won't be able to manage without it, and increasingly dubious about her ability to manage *with* it.

It's like when she was in high school and could never start her papers until the day before they were due. Mother or father always came to the rescue, helping her organize her thoughts or doing the typing for fear she would fail.

It takes a strong act of will to change a pattern like that. But it needs to be changed. Being on the giving end, even when no sacrifice is involved, makes you resentful. It automatically makes you feel you can sit in judgment. It obligates the children, encumbers them, makes them resentful, too. But, worst of all, it keeps them from leading their separate grown-up lives as best they can. Even when they long to be independent and responsible, it tends to make them feel incompetent and afraid to stand on their own, afraid of the consequences.

You may avoid this kind of situation if you try not to let your feelings of sympathy and anxiety for your daughter obscure the dollar-and-cents facts.

Try to make the discussion as businesslike as you can in the circumstances. Pretend you are investigating the merit of any loan request. What is it for? Why is it necessary? How and when can it be repaid? How can it solve the underlying financial problem so that the emergency will not recur?

If you want to give the money outright and can afford to, fine. If you feel the request is justified and prefer lending, agree on the period of the loan, the date and period for repayment, the interest rate, if any.

Then *forget* the gift. *Forget* the loan until due.

Be careful not to use your help as justification for intruding in your daughter's life. Don't make it an excuse for asking favors and attention, demanding accounting for expenditures, criticizing management, and so on.

When the loan is due, accept it and compliment her on the efficiency with which she has managed. Don't forgive the loan. Leave the slate clean. That makes it easy for her to ask again if she needs to, and easier for you to respond, if you want to.

Loans or gifts for home purchases or business investment are a bit easier than loans for survival purposes. The mere request signals, in a way, that a child is moving in the traditionally accepted upward direction. Some parents like to give their children money they have to spare when the children's needs are greatest, rather than will it to them. If you're one of these, fine. Others would rather lend their children the money they need for a business venture or the down payment on a home. In either case, the first step is to investigate the merits, as you would with any business proposition you might be offered.

Separate the facts in the case from the feelings that the request arouses. Explore the financial viability of the project. What you should try to avoid, in our opinion, is using your personal feelings about the child's need for your support as the basis for deciding to advance the money. Most children would welcome your sound business judgment about an investment they want to make, or the potential resale value of a house they have their eyes on. It's fine to point out that the zipper future is black. It's irrelevant to give your views on the partner's manners, or your opinion of the social status of zipper manufacturing. It's one thing to point out that a prospective home has rotten sashes and termites and is too close to the business district. It's another to say it's ugly, or that the neighbors look seedy.

It's obviously wise to discourage an investment that looks financially shaky, but don't use a request for help as an excuse to impose your standards, taste, and values. At the same time, don't withhold advice and encourage a child in a bad deal because you think you shouldn't say no.

Marriage

It may be safer to keep out of your children's private lives, especially their marital affairs, but it deprives parents, particularly mothers, of one of the nicer dividends of a good parent-child relationship: the pleasure of telling all about your own lives and hard/good times. Parents can be forgiven for wanting to share wisdom and experience. You can't help enjoying the feeling that someone you love may profit from your gains and losses—even if the feeling is illusory. Parents who are interested and involved give daughters a warm feeling in the spot where serenity and anxiety both grow. Once a child, always a child. Knowing that someone loves and understands you "as is" is a durable and unique source of comfort. Children, whatever their age, always want it, always miss it when it's gone.

Mixing in, we feel, is not only okay but splendid— provided you do it with sensitivity. Wait for an invitation, don't enter without knocking, know when to decline an offer to come in, have sense enough to know when to go home, be careful not to take over the premises.

Young married children used to love collecting their mothers' recipes, cures for croup, and secrets for taking out stains. They still do, but they also ask for a lot of brand-new kinds of advice: How can I get my husband to be a more

207

active father? What do you think of a day-care center for the baby instead of a live-in nurse? How can I ever be sure of what I want to do? I want to go back to work. All my friends are. I hate to leave the baby. I can't decide whether I'm reacting to trendy pressures or personal guilt. Help me!

Daughters talk more openly about marriage and the problems that come up in the early years as they begin to wake from the inevitable dream of total mutuality, instant comfort, complete happiness.

On first thought, advice for recipes and advice about marriage would seem to have very little in common. You could hardly go wrong on a cake recipe—short of leaving out the flour. The hazards of opening your mouth about marriage seem infinite. But examine more thoughtfully and you'll find that you can go just as wrong with a cake recipe as you can with marriage counseling.

Just take the cake, for example. You give the ingredients, the mixing, beating, and baking instructions; add whatever wisdom you've learned from experience, such as don't over-beat, or warm the butter. That's it. You can also, as some do, use the occasion to criticize the quantity of cake con-sumption in your daughter's family, the children's table manners, or her household management, or, worse yet, offer to take over for her until she learns—and see where you'd be.

As a parallel illustration, take the husband. Your daugh-ter complains that he puts her down. Suggesting possible causes for the husband's unfortunate behavior, reminiscing about your experience when you suffered similarly, suggest-ing remedies you found successful, suggesting that love and humor may bring him out of it, is all fine advice. Going from there to a discussion of the husband's cosmic weaknesses, your daughter's provocative habits, and your deep-seated fears and hesitancies about the marriage is dangerous, of course.

Avoid letting personal feelings and opinions get into the dialogue. As in discussions of money, stick to the point and the relevant facts. Offer specific advice based on your experience and knowledge of human relations. Minimize rather than build up the problem. Living together—no matter how long it lasts—requires constant, endless adjustment. Try to give your daughter some of the perspective that living and looking back must give you. Help her to pick her issues: settle the big ones and forget the tiny ones.

A sample: your daughter calls from the office with nothing much to say—dull day, late night, everything's quiet, nothing much doing, both children are well for a change. She mentions that Joe, the bastard, left the house yesterday without putting his dishes in the dish washer when he knew she had to be ready for an early meeting. When she reminded him at night he said she acted as if she were the only person in America who had a job.

The correct response from you is, "Umm. Was my friend from Jones, Ltd., at your meeting?" or "Daddy found that first edition of the Fitzgerald book you wanted."

Joe may sound horrible, nasty, but don't say so. This very night he may be up with the baby five times, while your daughter sleeps right through. If you get involved, then when you talk to each other tomorrow you'll be sure to ask, "Has Joe been any more understanding?" And you'll get a very cold, keep-out-of-my-business kind of reply, like, "You never did like Joe, did you?"

That's not to criticize your daughter, really. It's just to remind you how sensitive and volatile the marital relationship is, and to advise you against running the risk of mistaking passing feelings for profound maladjustment and dislocation. When your daughter reports her husband's petty transgressions, play deaf or laugh them off. That will make it clear to her that you are not in the complaint department.

When and if there are persistent serious problems, you'll hear about them. If you do, think twice before taking sides, in spite of entreaties for help and support. Sympathize, naturally. If you think your own experience might be helpful, talk about it. If you have any advice you think would be useful, offer it. If you can't advise or don't want to, find professional help.

It's flattering to be invited to aid and comfort—as if you were an expert. It's therefore easy to get carried away by the sound of your own voice. If you're not careful you can find yourself making sweeping judgments and offering Olympian solutions for difficult, complex problems. It's really safer and sounder, at first, to listen more and talk less. Solutions come slowly. Perhaps the most effective first step would be to give your daughter a chance to look at her situation more dispassionately, see the issues more clearly and try to find solutions on her own. If she remains defeated, then you might guide her to reputable marital counseling.

Try to preserve the privacy of your daughter's relations with her husband, even though it is sometimes hard when she is discouraged and needs comfort. If you can deal with her as another adult, rather than as a still-helpless child, you will make it easier for her to manage her life in the future. You will also find it easier, when—as often happens—the problems do get resolved, to resume a close and comfortable relationship with both her and your son-in-law.

Sons-in-law

The perennial in-law joke didn't just happen. It is firmly grounded in parents' wary posture toward their precious sons' and daughters' suitors. Mothers take more kindly to sons-in-law than to their sons' would-be wives. Same-sex suitors may be seen as rivals, so opposite-sex intruders usually get a warmer welcome. However, normal families, whatever their initial reaction, gradually let the outsiders into the inner circle and may eventually treat them even better than the natives.

Fathers start out with a "show me" attitude toward men who are interested in their daughters. Their sensitively tuned antennae often sniff impending nuptials before either of the parties has acknowledged their feelings toward each other. While protesting their fondness, admiration, and complete approval, fathers may privately express doubts about sons-in-law and/or lovers-in-law, and question their ability to measure up to daughters in character, virtue, charm, ability, achievement, or potential. Fortunately for family peace, mothers may err on the side of generosity. They inflate as fathers denigrate, and reasonably balanced judgments and marital harmony are thus achieved.

Ironically, when young families settle down and the in-law spouse has become more or less old-shoe, the mother-in-law may be more of a problem than the father-in-law. Mothers-in-law may overextend themselves with sons-in-law. Nostalgically, they romanticize as they once did with their own husbands—building a perfectly nice, regular, reasonably intelligent, decent fellow into a combination Hercules, Adonis, and mental giant, with tycoon potential.

Try not to fall in love with your son-in-law. He's taken. Acquiring new children by marriage is pleasant, even stimulating. It shifts arrangements just enough to change the mix and add zest to family life even when family life has been moving along smoothly and pleasantly for years. Enthusiasm, however, can go too far. It's lovely to like your daughter's husband, but don't have *his* favorite meal every time they come to dinner or plan all family gatherings to suit *his* interests. Above all, don't side with him or protect him.

If your daughter asks her husband for help, don't help him. Don't cluck and coo and tell him to sit still, commenting on how tired he must be at the end of his long day. (How would you feel if you were his hard-working wife?)

If your daughter asks him to go marketing with her, don't offer to go instead. She may simply be scheming for a few minutes alone with him, away from home and children and —face it—you.

If she complains to you about something he's said or how he said it, don't explain for him: "He didn't mean it" or "It didn't sound that way to me."

Know when to go for a walk, if you have been a house guest for a few days. Make a point of taking the grandchildren (if there are any) out for a treat, or a game of catch or jacks, or a museum visit. Ask how you can help, instead of butting in, countermanding instructions, or taking over.

No matter how happy and harmonious your relations with your children's families, don't force closeness.

No matter how regularly you may have been invited for a Sunday visit, don't assume you'll be invited *next* Sunday. Never pop in uninvited. If you're invited to visit children out of town, learn to judge when to leave—even if your invitation has not expired. Having outsiders around to think about, even when they're loved and wanted, is a strain, especially for young couples who work and have children to attend to at night.

You can avoid hurt feelings and hard feelings if you preserve a certain formality in all your relations. If your children drop in when they're in the neighborhood, drop off a child when they're going to a party nearby, have keys and drop in to borrow tools, utensils, equipment whether you're home or not, the time is bound to come when you won't like the intrusion, the borrowing, the imposition. You don't have to sit down and draw up rules together. Just establish them as you go along. If they come for a visit at five and appear to be expecting dinner, apologize and explain that you're having leftovers, you're going to the movies, or whatever may be the case. Then say in pleasant fashion, "Let me know when you're coming, so we can plan, won't you, because we really want to see you."

Children can't help thinking parents are made for them alone. And, if you encourage them, they will continue to assume that they are almost the only thing in your lives. If true—fine. If false, make that clear. Then no one will feel neglected, offended, or abused.

Minimize unpleasant episodes. Try to put yourselves back in their place. Parents' lives are usually smoothing out just when their young married children's lives are becoming most demanding and stressful. Overlook. Excuse. Forget harsh words, reprimands, slights. Don't harbor grudges, or punish with silence as if your daughter were an unruly, incorrigible, ill-mannered child. Remember what you have only lately finished teaching her: agree to disagree. You can be friends without seeing eye to eye on all subjects.

Grandparenthood

In this case the myth is based entirely on facts. Grandchildren are indeed the greatest, for all the obvious reasons. They're not yours. You can have them when you want them —if you behave yourself reasonably well with their parents. And you can always take them back home when you're tired.

You can do lots more, depending on your energy, interests, and endurance. What more could any human being want of another?

Enjoy them. Bask in their generous, warming, undemanding love. Watch the miracle of growth without worrying about whether it's below average, above average, or best on the block, or what the future will bring. Take advantage of the opportunity to teach the one you like to think takes after you to do the things you loved to do at the same age. Nourish their insatiable curiosity in the unhurried fashion that grandparents alone are capable of. Indulge their clumsy efforts to help in the comforting knowledge that even if it takes twice as long to bake the cookies or cut the grass it doesn't happen often. Spoil them by satisfying their dreams when you can, if their parents approve. Take them on trips. Buy them extravagant toys they really need, lessons they crave.

Let them bring you closer to their parents, but be careful not to let them come between you and their mother.

They may be a particularly flawless addition to your life, but, to their parents, they are no more model, smart, obedient, manageable, than those parents seemed to you when they were children and you were sometimes tired young parents. Their parents will have many equally tired, discouraged, impatient, cross moments; nagging difficulties; and serious if passing problems.

When you live hundreds of miles apart and see your grandchildren on brief and well-spaced visits only, it's not very hard to take a semidetached view of parent-child relations. When you're in fairly constant touch with your children and watch what goes on in their families from day to day, it may be harder not to put your oar in. But the closer you are, the more important it is to mind your manners.

Don't give advice unless invited, and then cautiously.

Be careful not to countermand parents' orders in their

house or in their presence. Don't argue about how to handle the kids. Aside from creating tension with your daughter, you'll confuse the children, and encourage disobedience.

Don't use the children to satisfy your own ego. When and if you feel like fulfilling dreams with lavish gifts or privileges, consult their parents first. No sense in spending lots of money on clothes when all they wear is blue jeans and what they really need is books, records, or orthodontia.

When you love people, it's natural to want to help and be part of their lives. If you help where help is needed you'll be more appreciated and enjoy the helping more. It's a good idea to ask your daughter what she'd like you to do for her when you feel like doing. Taking the children for a weekend sleep-over so their parents can get up as late as they want and enjoy total freedom from responsibility for twenty-four hours may make everyone happier than another TV game or Barbie outfit for the child(ren).

You may love having all the grandchildren visit together, but it may be a bigger treat for children and parents to part with one at a time, particularly at peak periods of sibling rivalry. That way each child gets more individual attention from parents and grandparents—the ones they love the best.

How can you hold your tongue, when your daughter loses hers? Keep your perspective. When she slaps or scolds unfairly, ignore. If she seems upset about having lost her patience, remind her that mothers are people, too, no better and no worse than the rest of us. Remind her that children are also human—sometimes naughty, provocative, and disobedient when they know better.

Guilt sometimes makes people act even worse. They seem to have to punish themselves for being bad by acting worse. Relieve parents' guilt and you can sometimes feel the family climate clearing, minute by minute.

While it's good general policy to keep out of your married children's business, noninterference can sometimes be dangerous.

If you saw your ten-year-old grandson hitching a ride on the back of a city bus, or your thirteen-year-old granddaughter sipping gin with a pal in a secluded spot, you wouldn't stop to consider whether it would be right to butt in. You'd tell their parents fast. There are less dramatic moments when it is just as important to step in—whether it's interference or not.

You may not be quite the expert that you sometimes think you are, but you are more experienced than your children, particularly when they're beginning parents. You may also see your grandchildren with more objectivity.

You don't have to worry about whether you're imagining troubles that aren't there. In fact, grandparents can usually accept deviations from the ideal or average more easily than parents can. They've seen how much behavior can vary from one child to another and still be perfectly normal. They also know that the weather, next week's test, yesterday's accident, or last week's virus can create all kinds of temporary aberrations of body and spirit. They can tell the passing disturbance from the persistent problem or the behavior that gets worse rather than better with time.

If you are troubled by a mental, physical, or emotional problem that you have seen developing, unnoticed by parents, say so.

Wait for the right moment, when parents are not preoccupied and children are well out of earshot. You might express your concern as a question. "Have you ever thought that Jill might need glasses? She keeps asking what the bus ads say and I know they're words she knows," or "Has Sally's teacher ever commented on her work? Do you think she's reading up to her age level?"

Sometimes you may have to be more direct to get your

message across. Avoid making a firm diagnosis. You may alarm, unnecessarily. Don't say, "I think Jill is very near-sighted," or "I think Sally's retarded," or "Peter has a serious emotional problem, I'm sure."

Try to be circumspect: "I think it would be a good idea to check Sally's vision," or "Why don't you ask Peter's teacher whether he's having a good time at school? He acts so quiet these days—almost unhappy."

The problem might be the parents' rather than the child's. We knew a couple of young parents who entertained themselves with their five-year-old daughter's mental acrobatics. They pushed her to read and parrot math facts—all of which she would have learned in the first weeks of first grade. Meanwhile, as her grandfather noticed, little Joan was absolutely out of it with her playmates. She tried to teach them and boss them instead of playing. He advised her parents to redirect their teaching efforts for a while and explained why.

His daughter told him—not too politely—to mind his business. He reminded her that he probably cared as much about Joan and her welfare as they did, and just might have a point—based on longer and broader experience.

His daughter didn't apologize. A week later, however, she announced that she was taking Joan to a play group twice a week, "and she loves it."

If her parents continued their home classroom, Joan's grandparents never witnessed the lessons again. They did notice, however, that Joan was soon playing happily with the children next door.

Interfering isn't easy, even when it's necessary. Advice is often taken as criticism and resented or angrily rejected. Suggesting serious problems has to create acute fear. Like all of us, young parents often fight fear with anger and denial: "You scared me. It's not true."

When there's a potentially dangerous situation, however, your primary concern is the child's welfare. Make sure your message is clearly understood. Make sure there is some follow-up. It may help to remind your children that most problems respond more quickly and successfully when they are spotted early. If your concerns are groundless, you will all be relieved together. If they're well founded, both you and your children will be glad that you butted in. And to end on a brighter note, no child grows up problem-free, but very few problems are insoluble. And very few children have problems so serious that they can't live reasonably satisfying lives, problems or not.

CHAPTER TWELVE

What Fathers Are For

Human beings are born male and female, but they learn to be masculine and feminine—mannish and womanish—to suit the society they live in. In different times and places, men and women, both, have been aggressive or passive, dominating or submissive, independent or dependent, maternal or remote, affectionate or aloof. In the days when power was inherited, the need to ensure clear lines of succession kept women in virtual slavery. In preindustrial society the importance of physical strength for survival influenced sex roles. Modern technology has now made us almost interchangeable. Practically speaking, men and women could take each other's places, and do, except for procreational purposes.

But, while men's and women's roles change, changing is not necessarily smooth or easy.

Men, brought up to be heads of families, find the spot suddenly occupied—at least partly. It raises problems.

Who's the boss? Who does what? If man abdicates, or shares, who is he now? What does he do? Where does he stand?

Women, brought up to be mothers and wives, and trained to take a back seat—at least in public—are bringing home the mortgage money, not just the bacon. They're rising as fast as or faster than their husbands. Who's minding the children? Who calls the doctor? Who talks to the teacher? Who goes to the holiday plays? Who buys the birthday presents? Will day-care mother or housekeeper replace Mommy? Will Daddy? What's feminine? What's Father for?

There is a lot of conflict and confusion. But in the midst of it, there's a bright side. The disparity between yesterday's teaching and today's life may be causing you a certain amount of intermittent anguish, but the world is child's play to your children. Male or female—they're adaptable and accepting. They take what they're given, within reason. A whiff of the past here and there won't faze them. The mishmash of the society they're born into is natural to them. They'll choose the slot that fits and slip in as easily as a penny in a gum ball machine.

If you can go about your business, doing your job, taking your rest and relaxation, managing your household and family life to suit yourselves, and forget who's who and what's what in the tired old roles you were brought up with, your sons and daughters will be bound to benefit, with you.

Life with father was a major focus of the conversations about childhood that we had in preparation for this book. We asked women how they got along with their fathers, what role their fathers played in their care and guidance, what they remembered about their fathers with pleasure, how their fathers treated them, compared with their brothers, in terms of help, privileges, opportunities, and attention. We asked about their father and mother's relationship and about their fathers' influence on their grown-up lives.

Two of the more than thirty women remembered their fathers with unqualified affection and joy. We were unprepared for the predominantly negative outpouring from the rest. It is not accidental that the fictional American father is portrayed as a back-slapping, bullying sentimentalist on the one hand, and on the other as a shadowy, unapproachable figure around whom the family tiptoes in fear and constraint.

Memories were wistful and sad, rather than bitter. Young women, as often as older ones, regardless of their background and present adjustment, remembered themselves as little girls adoring a father whose attention and affection they were never sure of having or holding.

One girl asked her successful lawyer father about studying law. He smiled his father-at-daughter smile, asked her if she thought she'd look nice in robes and a wig, and called her Portia for a while. Until she was in college she actually believed that American women lawyers wore robes and wigs in court.

She was an eager participant in the dinner-table discussions of his cases, but he never suggested that she apply to law school. When she was the first woman to win an important graduate fellowship he teased her for studying what he called a "non-subject"—political science.

Daughters were part of the ambiance their mothers created for their fathers' rest and recreation. They were a kind of animated part of the décor. What they did—their marks, their achievements, their appearance, their manners, their reputations—was important only as it filled out a generally pleasing image of charm, grace, comfort, success, like their mothers' clothes, parties, social activities, and food.

A twelve-year-old girl expressed daughters' feelings about fathers as poignantly as anyone we talked to. "I know my father loved us. My parents wouldn't have had five children otherwise. He works very hard. He says yes to any kind of lesson, any school or camp any of us wants. But I want him to help me. Last year, for example, I was trying to learn geometry. He could have explained it so I'd understand. When I asked him he said, 'You try too hard. Don't be so serious. Marks aren't important.' Marks *are* important. But that wasn't the point. I want to learn. I'm interested in understanding. He's that way whenever I try to talk about anything serious. But I know he loves me."

Unresponsiveness to daughters is many-faceted. Girls learn to respond to the role their fathers set up for them. Or, if they are ambitious, curious, intellectually or creatively gifted, articulate, outgoing, and high-spirited, they learn to do without their fathers' love and approval. And they suffer varying degrees of conflict, confusion, and self-distrust, as a consequence.

Fathers are as important as mothers in making girls comfortable and confident. If a father rejects what a girl feels is important to her sense of herself, or makes fun of it or disapproves, it's trouble.

A girl whose father refused to support her plans for college said, "For ten years after I left home, whenever I began to feel serious about a boy I ran like hell. I was terrified of getting in that bind again. My father refused to take me seriously. It made me doubt myself for a long time. And any time I ever saw myself getting in the clutches of some guy I was scared to death he could destroy me too."

When someone as important as a young girl's much-loved father rejects what seems most basically herself, whether he makes fun, or disapproves or simply doesn't care, it's like Alice in Wonderland. She is; she is not. She keeps seesawing back and forth about who she really is—the person she presents to her father, or the person she senses her father wants to see. The conflict and confusion interfere with her behavior, the goals she sets, her performance and effort, her relations with men and women, and, finally, her own children.

Women also reported being sensitive to the way their fathers and mothers got along with each other.

Family stability and harmony were often maintained at the expense of their mothers' integrity. Mothers acquiesced in a system that required them to play dumb, submit to unjustified attack, and meekly allow their husbands to overrule them on issues as important as whether a daughter should be supported through college.

Girls suffered humiliation *with* their mothers. At the same time they sided *against* them. Perhaps it was less painful to be on the side of power than to identify with the helpless victims. The betrayal, however, generally tore them apart. Confusion in loyalties confused them about their identity as women.

The young woman whose father kept her mother from lending her money for college hated her father for humiliating her mother. But she was angrier at her mother for not defending herself. "She could scream and shout at him about something stupid like where to set the refrigerator controls, and sit there like a limp clam when something important came up," she told us.

A few years after this daughter graduated from college, her mother started a business with a friend, and succeeded. It was as much a victory for the daughter as for the mother. "Now I'm proud of her. Now we can talk like equals and be close."

Another young woman discussed her parents' divorce. Hers was a secure bourgeois life until she was eight. She was wrapped in comfort and love. Her father began having affairs, as was the custom in their level of Latin American society. What was not customary was her mother's refusal to accept the status quo. Neither could she accept her loss. She had a nervous breakdown and came home from the sanitarium permanently saddened. The little girl lived with her mother all week and spent her weekends on her father's yacht with a changing company of his toadying admirers, male and female. Her father showed her off. He complained if her clothes didn't suit him. He complained because she didn't smile enough. She often pretended to be sick on Fridays, but her mother forced her to go. She loved her father but also hated him for leaving them. She couldn't love her mother, who was so defeated and helpless. She really still loved them both. She grew up with one goal: "Independence. Never let a man get control." She feels that power is the key to survival, and closeness is synonymous with helplessness.

While a great deal of research has been directed toward finding out how little boys and girls become the kinds of men and women they do, it has produced very little solid data. Our own experience and observation probably tell us as much about the dynamics of human development as science ever will. First, children develop because they're made that way. Mental and emotional and physical development all go on at once and are obviously interrelated. A child has to be neurologically mature enough before she can sit up, as well as physically strong enough to master the task. Environment influences and shapes development, too. A child in an empty room can't learn to climb, even though physically and mentally prepared. A child who never hears language will never talk.

The physical and human environment influences development. But children are not simply imprinted by the world.

Their individuality determines, to a certain extent, what they learn and how they learn it, and the world affects their individuality as they learn. Learning is a complex process of interaction.

On the simplest, active level, children learn by imitating. Even before they can talk you will hear them babbling in such clear sentences—sounding so much like their mother, father, nurse, or sister—that you know right away they're copying.

You will see a tiny little boy or girl who has just learned to walk sit down on a couch next to father or mother and very painfully—watching the parent carefully all the time—cross his or her legs just like the grownup.

Imitation becomes ever more elaborate with age. Threes and fours of either sex imitate their fathers shaving and their mothers putting on lipstick and powder. They imitate the routines of daily life in play—getting breakfast, getting the children off to school, going to work.

Gradually imitation becomes more sophisticated. As children grow, they go beyond copying routines, the externals of life. They line themselves up with the parent of the appropriate sex and begin to imitate more accurately—to make that parent's image, as they see it, part of their own developing self-image. The mother is the primary parent from whom a daughter draws her view of herself, but her father is also directly and indirectly important in this process.

Girls grow up human, as well as feminine. You influence what they aim for, what they try, what they think about, how hard they try. You influence values, taste, wit, and thousands of other particularities about them just as much as the mother, the child's other first love, does, and just as other important people do later on.

Your influence asserts itself in different ways. You influence them by what you are without consciously teaching them. If you allow them to, they will choose what they want to take from you, according to their natures. In a more complicated way, you influence the way they come to perceive themselves as women. They watch you as they watch their mothers for clues to tell them what women are supposed to be, what women are worth.

The way you are together influences them: how you relate to each other and how you relate to your daughter. Children like to grow up to be what you expect them to be. Girls get the image of womanhood from the way their mothers look to them and what their mothers approve in them. They also get their picture of what to be from the way they see themselves reflected in their fathers' reactions to them and from the way their fathers relate to their mothers.

Most fathers don't set out deliberately to hurt their daughters. They just do what comes naturally, as their fathers did before them. They fill roles they have been taught just as they put on the clothes their mothers laid out for them when they were very little boys. Their roles were designed to serve a purpose—and they did, at one time. They taught men to protect and shield women and provide for them and the children who would carry on.

The rules worked; and while they did, they served men and women equally well. Men gained power in return for taking risks and assuming responsibility. Women gained security and support in return for service. Now the roles are irrelevant. Men don't guarantee women protection and security. They can't. Women must learn to be responsible for themselves in self-defense.

Gradually women have become conscious, and begun to make men aware, that times are changing. Men now know what they are giving up. Since power is the name of the game in our society, no one wants to yield it. Those who feel their hold on it is shaky go to extreme lengths to convince themselves and others that they are more powerful than ever. The intelligent man who lectures on the financial waste of educating women; the father who waits up for his eighteen-year-old daughter to get home with her date; the man who spanks his two-year-old son for getting into his mother's makeup, or tells his high school senior he can't study art because it's effeminate, acts out of desperation.

Like most maladaptive behavior, it doesn't work. You can't turn back the clock or bury technology. It doesn't work for marriage (women, as the divorce statistics show, can make it alone, in the interest of self-preservation). It ill prepares children of both sexes for the future. It makes men defensive, deceptive, and unreachable, as if they were saying, "If they get beyond my public posture they'll find me empty and unarmed."

You can't be friends if you're not real. You can't love if you don't reveal. You can't sympathize, comfort, and respond—or be a real whole person—if you can't let yourself be yourself. Clinging to a hollow power makes you really lonely and powerless. Indirectly, it deprives women of their selves and children of the love and support they need from you to become people themselves. It deprives you of them.

As sex roles converge, men may lose some power, but men and women will both gain some humanity. No longer obliged to scrunch, squeeze, and adapt to the requirements of obsolete roles they can begin to cultivate and celebrate themselves. Being themselves, they can be more human. They can relate more humanly to their children.

As long as you have to trim your feelings, cultivate your interests and tastes, and develop skills to suit a trumped-up masculinity, you will inevitably teach your children to do the same. You will teach them to conceal some feelings, hide some fears (if they're boys), pretend some fears (if they're girls), suppress some interests, fake others, and so on. You will inhibit their natural development. They will grow up with whole chunks of their emotional, imaginative, creative, expressive selves painfully suppressed, distorted, or quite left out.

If you are free to be yourself, you will be free to be human. You can be both motherly and fatherly, tender and protective, strong and independent. You can respond to your children, humanly, as the need demands, and thus you will encourage them to grow humanly—to realize themselves as individuals, and express themselves as men or women, in their individual ways.

Chris, a twenty-five-year-old unmarried office worker, is one of the two women we interviewed who thinks her father is absolutely splendid. He works for the Sanitation Department in New York City. Her mother never worked at all. In this family of Italian extraction machismo was as traditional as pasta. But it was strictly for show. Chris's brother was a terror as a child. He got away with it. He didn't help her mother. His father wouldn't have allowed it. Chris got better marks. No one was impressed. Her brother got kicked out of school. Her father said, "What do you expect of a boy?" But he made it clear it would not happen again.

However, in high school, when other girls' fathers refused to let them out, or sat up to bawl out their dates when they got home fifteen minutes late, her father never made a rule. He trusted her. Both children knew their father expected them to go to college. Her brother finally made it on his own after working for a year and finding out what he wanted to study. She took a summer job after high school and liked it too much to quit for college. But she's determined to get the preparation she needs to teach before she marries, because she knows it takes two salaries these days to live the way she wants to live.

"When I marry I'll have children and I'll want to stay

with them as my mother did. It's not the end of life. It's only a few years. I had friends whose mothers worked. They were lonely. I'll work when my children go to school all day.

"My father and mother are old-fashioned, I guess. That's the way they were brought up. My marriage will be different, of course, but I hope I find a man who treats me the way my father treats my mother. They're friends. He helps her with everything. It's never 'You do this,' 'I only do this.' They don't even seem to be working when they clean the house. They talk and laugh all the time. They never act bored. They have fights. But it's over in a minute. They were so easy to grow up with. It wasn't rules and punishment. It just seemed to be expected that we'd turn out like they did—okay. You know, we still sit there and look at the dumb movies my father took—every weekend in the park. We still like remembering."

When you see what a good father means to a girl, it makes it easier to be one.

This book assumes that fathers and mothers will bring up their children together. However, fathers have their particular roles to play with daughters, and we have tried to indicate how they influence a girl's development every step of the way, from infancy to maturity. Here, in summary, are the principal do's and don'ts. They are not absolute and binding, just guidelines to help you find your own way to be a father.

DO get into the act from the start. Feeding, bathing, dressing, changing a baby, is the very best way to get to know her and her needs and find out how you can meet them best. Taking care makes you care.

DON'T say things like "Here's your daughter" and hand her to her mother when she's dirty, cross, or hungry or you just want to watch TV. Girls need two full-time parents if they are to grow up sure of themselves as women. If you push her off on her mother when she's inconvenient, you tell her that you can take her or leave her. You tell her mother that you come first and mothers and daughters come second. Your daughter needs to know she can depend on you, that you care for her—for better or worse.

DO bring her up from babyhood to feel that her options are as wide open as her brother's—limited only by her abilities, interests, efforts, and desires. Over the years we've been able to watch life change on a New England farm. We saw today's farmer, as a toddler, learn to steer a tractor in his father's lap. Last spring we watched his little daughter learn to steer the tractor in *his* lap.

DO give your daughter the experiences that will stimulate her imagination. Satisfy her curiosity. Play and teach.

DON'T be a formula father. If you like fooling with cars, let her watch and ask questions and help. Don't try to teach her chess or take her to art galleries because you think it would be good for her. Let her see you at your best—involved, enthusiastic, interested. That's what gives her the will to try and to dream. Then she'll find her own interests to pursue.

DO treat her as an individual. Forget the "sugar and spice and everything nice" clichés. What we all hope for in our children is an expectant, curious, lively, unafraid approach to life. Demure, polite, pink-cheeked, smiling, golden-haired girls are nice. But if you think of your daughter as a person with a future, rather than a picture-book child, you will enjoy her vim, vigor, daring, and inquisitiveness as much as her sweetness and charm.

DON'T teach her to use guile and wiles to get her way. Of course, all parents let all children beat them down *sometimes,* flattering, coaxing, whining, wheedling, finding the soft spot. But try not to teach your daughter that you're a pushover for her and tough with your son.

DO teach her to be responsible.

DON'T spoil her.

DO set standards to suit the child, according to age and individual capacity. Then, making allowance for human frailty, see that girls conform as dutifully as boys.

DON'T blame sons when daughters provoke them by teasing, or interfering with their work or play, and they retaliate in self-defense. Don't expect boys to be "easy" on little sisters or big ones. Don't let girls "get away with it" whether "it" is forgetting work, goofing off, being "tired" at the moment of truth, blaming someone or something, or playing "daddy's girl."

DO bring up your sons and daughters, both, to be human. Looks, style, taste, charm, femininity, are as much a part of a girl as drive, determination, goals, talents, ability, ideas.

DON'T exchange the old "sugar and spice" stereotype for the "I have to be the first woman president" one. Bring your daughter up to realize herself according to her individual capacities and interests, and accept herself as fully as possible—her body, emotions, and sensuality as well as her aspirations.

DO teach your daughter to value herself by paying attention to her needs, questions, interests—her *self*. Enjoy her and her friends, male and female.

DO let her choose her friends by herself. If she learns to feel important and worthy, she'll be less likely to remake herself to please others, to be popular. If she has a chance to make her own choice of friends and see how her judgment works, she'll probably learn to be a pretty good judge of people in the end.

DON'T scout her boy friends, challenge them, interrogate them, get a verbal résumé from each one. Leave them to her.

DO check your patriarchal stance now and then.

DON'T set different social standards for boys and girls.

DON'T keep girls from being responsible by protecting them from responsibility. Don't wait up for them when you don't wait up for their brothers. Don't assume they are unable to protect themselves. Be sure they know how. Don't judge them by old standards of behavior, but trust them as you know them.

DO avoid making class pronouncements about women.

DON'T put women down at home or abroad. Avoid "lousy woman driver" when the lady in front of you turns without signaling. Don't make fun of your wife when she makes an error in the checkbook—particularly when she does the balancing. Don't ridicule your sister when she attempts to make a business judgment affecting you.

DON'T belittle women for being soft, tender, sentimental, sensitive, and motherly.

DON'T belittle *yourself* for being soft, tender, sentimental, sensitive, and motherly.

DO try to show her that good and bad, weakness and strength, talents and abilities, are shared equally by both the sexes, and encourage her to choose her friends and loves to suit her rather than to suit stereotypes—sexual or social.

DO support her expectations of her future self, by supporting her mother as wife, mother, and woman, now. If you can't bring her up in harmony together, bring her up in harmony apart. But try to stay together as parents.

DON'T blame your wife for your problems—joint or separate.

DON'T use your child as a weapon.

DON'T abandon your daughter with your marriage.

CHAPTER THIRTEEN

Mothers and Daughters

Bind or Bond

The new mother puts her baby daughter to rest. For the thousandth time she lingers to study the little features, soft in sleep. She feels a kind of love she has never known before. The newborn child can stir the most solemn resolves in even the most unsolemn mother.

They range from reverent to ridiculous. This darling daughter will never have to eat spinach. This perfect child won't be forced to go to college when what she wants to do is dance. She will never be compared with her siblings—if any—particularly invidiously. If she's shy, no one will ever make her speak up, say "please," or have the party at her house. She won't be made to get out of the water until *she* says she's cold.

New motherhood brings back long-forgotten scenes from childhood. Pleasure and pain, triumph and defeat, glory and grief, achievement and frustration, dreams and despair are vivid again. New mothers may remember the way they were, the way they felt, and the way they wished it was when they were still just daughters, and vow and believe they will eliminate all their own mothers' mistakes.

Fortunately, as the baby grows, walks, screams, stomps her foot, and learns to say "NO" fluently, she becomes a little less holy and more human. The initial vows become less sacred. Mothers learn to make their peace with perfection. The resolves made in the early, innocent days of motherhood gradually get lost in the shuffle of everyday reality. The sweet, soft, sleepy, hungry, smily little baby—as malleable as Silly Putty—becomes a force to be considered. She has too many sniffles. She won't pick up her toys or let you out of her sight. She needs more friends. She wants to read and nursery school won't let her. She gives up too easily. She never gives up. She stretches out bedtime to infinity. She loves her nursemaid, father, grandmother, or day-care giver more than she does her mother. Is it wrong to work? Is it wrong to stay home? Should a mother be so cross? When should you say no? Is it right not to read her a story when she dallies instead of getting ready for bed? If you don't read it, will you delay reading readiness? Make her feel rejected? If you do, won't it spoil her? How *do* you civilize a child without squelching her?

Sometimes mothers feel like high-wire artists threading their way through an aerial maze. Each step demands such total concentration that they are in constant danger of forgetting their goal and losing the way. Amazingly enough, they seldom do. Most mothers get to know their babies. They learn to adapt to them. They develop a refined and delicate sense of when to push, when to pull, when to prompt, when to retire, when to *make* responsible, when to *be* responsible. Through the infinitude of exchanges that go on day after day, week after week, year after year, they teach their children how to find their way in the world. In spite of the inevitable compromises with their early oaths of office, they continue to take motherhood seriously. They want to do their best and their best is usually very good indeed.

When mothers fail their daughters it is, most often, when they are not even aware of what they are doing. Women's roles, goals, and options have changed radically in the last ten years. If current trends continue, your daughter will probably work most of her life to support herself or help support her family. She may have total responsibility for her children during some part of their early lives. She will have choices that her grandmother could not have imagined.

These changes have not all happened suddenly. Women's horizons have been expanding steadily in recent generations. But, although expectations of daughters have changed accordingly, parents have continued to bring up girls as if nothing has happened. Young women who are not yet mothers and others who are just starting to have children have learned to define themselves as women in much the same way their grandmothers did—and their grandmothers before them.

Girls are still trained to be wives and mothers first. Parents still teach them to be modest, unassuming, and retiring; to please men rather than to satisfy themselves; to put others' needs and interests before their own.

Little girls, like little boys, are sensual, affectionate, curious about themselves and their environment, experimental, and assertive. These are human characteristics. They are there for a purpose. They help children develop the courage, initiative, and will to master their environment, survive, and reproduce. Traditionally, girls in Western society have been taught to suppress these qualities, to be afraid of their feelings and impulses and ashamed of expressing themselves spontaneously and directly. Understanding how this happens and thinking hard about how it has affected you can help you break out of the pattern, and raise your daughters differently.

How do you feel about feelings? Your body? How do you feel about speaking up for yourself? Guilty or comfortable? How do you feel about acknowledging ambitions? Can you control your life? Or do things just happen to you? Do you want to give your daughter freedom of choice in her life? Or does the idea make you vaguely uncomfortable? Do you have a fixed image of what she ought to be?

Perhaps some of the stories of childhood told us by the women we have talked with will help you remember how you arrived where you are now. Perhaps remembering will help you change your ways and bring up your daughter for her times.

Over and over we heard how little girls began to fear their feelings and finally to be afraid of themselves.

Here is a woman with grown-up children who holds an important academic post in a university, recalling an incident from her toddler days:

"My mother was bathing me. She gave me a special washcloth and pointed to my vagina. Then—as if she were telling me to clean up a mess I'd made—she said, 'Wash down there. Be very careful. If you don't keep it clean, it will get sore. It's very delicate.'

"I didn't dare ask her what 'it' was. Instinctively, I guess, I knew it was the nice part. Now it wasn't nice any more. It was something I shouldn't have. I felt it, anyway. But it scared me. I began to think there was something bad about that feeling. I felt guilty.

"Later I was sure. My father had this very tall, handsome friend who used to ride my brother and me on his shoulders when he came. He called it flying. My mother always stopped him when it was my turn—if she was around. 'Don't throw her!' she'd say, very urgently. 'She'll get hurt.'

"I wasn't afraid. I felt safe and powerful and free. I think I knew that lovely feeling was what she didn't want me to have."

The so-called sexual revolution hasn't changed this training. A young woman artist remembered asking her mother if she had a little thing like her own clitoris. "She told me to eat my potatoes and never talk about things like that. I felt so bad. If she had slapped me I couldn't have hurt more. So unexpected."

A young financial analyst remembered a scene from her life as an eight-year-old tomboy in a neighborhood where boys were the only playmates available. One day when she came home from school her mother was waiting, stern, unsmiling. "She told me that all the boys' mothers were talking about me because I had come out of Peter's house when Peter's mother wasn't home. We'd been trading baseball cards. I didn't know what she was upset about, but I realized I had disgraced her. I felt hot and shamed and helpless all at once. It was the end of my fun for a long time. I just never knew when I might do the strange, bad thing she was so upset about. She could have told me a few things instead of scaring me like that. I kept wondering what I had done or might do that was so terrible, and I ended up finally feeling that there was something innately bad in me."

Little girls reported feeling very early that there was something bad in their bodies connected with pleasure. They learned to feel guilty for wanting the pleasant feelings that they sometimes couldn't prevent, guilty when they allowed themselves to enjoy them, and finally afraid of feeling at all. The pleasure became a guilty secret they tried to conceal, even from themselves, with imperfect success.

Thus spontaneity of feeling was curbed. Next, expressiveness, assertiveness, girls' natural interest in excelling and achieving—in becoming a person—were discouraged. Learning how to be a girl meant learning, once again, that the way that seemed natural to them was somehow unnatural.

In her thirteenth summer a girl who is now doing research in biochemistry was working on a play with a friend. Out of the summer silence she overheard a friend of her mother's on the porch below her room: "Theo is too smart. Johnny says the boys are afraid of her." That night when she came down to help with dinner her mother looked at her as if she had a terminal illness. "I had always thought she enjoyed my interest and success in school and liked to hear my ideas for plays and stories. I even thought she was proud of me. I had been perfectly happy with myself. When I found that being popular with boys was what really counted for her, my comfort just disappeared. I was lonely and self-conscious for years. In graduate school I met people who cared about what I did. It was like being reborn. Finally I could be myself."

Of course, not all women suffer that dramatically. They simply learn to stop talking to their mothers about things they care about. They talk instead about what matters to their mothers: their friends, their progress in tennis, how much piano practicing they've done, who's having parties, whether they're invited. Their mothers don't necessarily alter the course of their lives. Inevitably, though, they become different people than they might have been. They develop less trusting, intimate relationships with their mothers than they might have if their mothers had been able to meet them where they were and take them seriously. And the conflict and confusion and self-doubt that their childhood training in womanhood creates forms their adult behavior.

Some play their traditional roles faithfully on the surface.

But their frustrated drives and feelings pop out in perverse ways.

As anyone with a smattering of popular psychological wisdom or just plain human insight knows, you don't erase an individual's basic nature and drives by saying "go 'way." You can frown, scold, and punish severely. You may effectively suppress the proscribed behavior, but you don't really wipe out the drives and impulses behind it. The drives fight a constant battle to escape the built-in controls that keep them in check. So women's behavior often reflects the changing course of that inner strife.

Women have difficulty asserting themselves directly and appropriately, both at home and at work. They crumple when they should defend themselves to bosses. They intimidate subordinates. If they stay home, their drives escape furtively. One minute they are running their husbands' careers, or running them down. The next they allow themselves to be browbeaten and abused.

They're not dependable. They assume responsibilities and scare when pressures get heavy. Ambition and drive are dangerous: they make women feel guilty and weak. Too much assertiveness, too much responsibility, force women to retreat to their stereotypes and let others bail them out. They make excuses: husbands disapprove; children need them.

In their helplessness the will to assert themselves constantly resurfaces. They push their own daughters to realize their frustrated dreams. Then they give them conflicting, unclear, unpredictable messages. They encourage enterprise and assertiveness one minute, then caution against making *ripples* the next. They want daughters to achieve for *them*. They want success through their daughters. They find it hard to allow daughters to grow and achieve for themselves —to be independent. They want them to succeed as long as

241

they are pretty, quiet, pleasing to men, devoted to children, and womanly in the way womanly was defined for *them*. They want and believe in freedom for their daughters, but often they lack the courage to let them go.

Their conflicting messages interfere with their girls' healthy development and make it hard for them to figure out how to be women. As models, they can make being a woman seem unappealing, if not fearsome. In spite of their loving devotion and their will to do their best, they are too often helpless when they should be strong, dominating when they should let go, discouraging when they could be supportive. They give up when they should stand fast, and stand fast when they should bend.

Women's responsibilities have changed enormously already. Men's and women's expectations of each other are changing. To succeed in the lives that will be theirs and take advantage of their new opportunities, girls need to be free of the restrictive lessons from our childhoods. They need to be assertive. They do need to be in touch with their bodies and their feelings. They do need to be courageous enough to make decisions and take responsibility for them. They need mothers who can give them clear signals and dependable guidance and provide encouraging evidence of the possibility and promise there is in being a woman. Think about the child you were and the influences that make you the woman you are. Being aware of yourself will help you give your daughter the kind of example and guidance that will make her path to a new kind of maturity as a woman much easier.

No matter how old a woman is or how long she has been a mother, in some deep, changeless part of her she remains her mother's daughter. When a mother sows distrust, fear, confusion, uncertainty, she binds her daughter forever in a complex tangle of childish dependency, love, and resentment that never lets her go to be wholeheartedly herself. When a mother can be a fairly reliable model of love and generosity, understanding and forbearance, strength and courage, the everlasting quality of the mother-daughter relationship can be a lifelong source of comfort, strength, and continuity to her daughter as she goes about her separate, independent life. Fortunate the mother and daughter whose bond helps build a bridge to the future.

Index

A